Sentence Composing

The Complete Course

Sentence Composing

The Complete Course

DON KILLGALLON
Baltimore County Schools

BOYNTON/COOK PUBLISHERS, INC.
UPPER MONTCLAIR, NEW JERSEY 07043

Library of Congress Cataloguing-in-Publication Data

Killgallon, Don.
  Sentence composing.

  1. English language—Sentences. 2. English
language—Composition and exercises. 3. English
language—Rhetoric. I. Title.
PE1441.K53 1986   808′.042   86-14757
ISBN 0-86709-183-5

For information address Boynton/Cook Publishers, Inc.
52 Upper Montclair Plaza, P.O. Box 860, Upper Montclair, NJ 07043

Printed in the United States of America.

87 88 89 90 91 10 9 8 7 6 5 4 3 2 1

Preface

SENTENCE COMPOSING: *The Complete Course* emphasizes the most neglected unit of written composition: the sentence. Using four techniques—*sentence scrambling, sentence imitating, sentence combining,* and *sentence expanding*—the book teaches students structures they seldom use in their writing, but should and can easily use once they become familiar with them through many examples and practices.

The book concentrates on such structures by means of model sentences by professional writers. The rationale is based on the widely accepted mimetic theory of *oral* language acquisition, applied here to *written* language acquisition in the belief that continual exposure to structures used often by professionals in their sentences will produce attention to, understanding of, and, with practice, normal use of such structures by students in their sentences.

The book is an exercise in applied grammar, with theory and terminology of grammar subordinate to the major goal, composing sentences. The naming of parts and the parsing of sentences, the goals of traditional grammar study, are exercises in dissection. The practices in SENTENCE COMPOSING are exercises in production.

The four sentence composing techniques are easily learned. The practices based on them are interesting and challenging, and they can be done by any student. In addition, the teacher can readily give attention to the sentences students compose, with quicker, more constant, and more thorough feedback than with longer compositions.

Since the practices have proved successful for the great majority of students who have used them in all kinds of schools, it's demonstrably true that SENTENCE COMPOSING can work anywhere—in any school, with any student.

To students: the best, the brightest, the baddest, but, most of all, to all the others—the ones for whom nothing ever seems to work.

Contents

Introduction:
How Sentence Composing Works

How do professional writers learn to write their sentences? Often, ironically, not through writing but through reading. Good writers are also good readers. When professional writers read, they don't just read for meaning; they read for style, including how good sentences are composed. Their writing school is the pages between the covers of a book, and their writing teachers are the authors of those pages—the best writing teachers available. Unconsciously or consciously, good writers learn to write through imitation.

SENTENCE COMPOSING is based upon a similar process: learning by imitating. The theory that imitation is the sincerest form of flattery is rooted in the theory that imitation is often the best form of learning. Great writers of the past were routinely schooled in the imitation of master writers, often copying verbatim from their writings, hoping something would rub off. Many (including Shakespeare) learned the craft of writing partly through imitation. The same method, applied to composing sentences, is used exclusively in SENTENCE COMPOSING. This textbook is based on the principle that learning to compose good sentences can be greatly aided through the deliberate imitation of professionally written sentences.

In most grammar and writing textbooks since the nineteenth century, almost no use has been made of imitation, one of the methods used to teach writing in earlier times, even though that method proved effective. Common from the Renaissance through the nineteenth century, sentence imitation has largely been neglected in favor of sentence analysis. The diagramming, labeling, and classifying of sentences has been paramount. The hope was that sentence analysis would improve the composing of sentences, that "knowing" would result in "doing." Students learned how to analyze sentences, but not how to improve their own. SENTENCE COMPOSING reverses the emphasis and the order, with imitation receiving major attention and analysis minor attention, with "doing" resulting in "knowing," on the assumption that imitating the sentences of professional writers also yields useful knowledge about grammar, about words, and about writing.

This is not a grammar book. Whether you can compose good sentences is the main concern of the textbook, not whether you can identify grammatical structures. The practices in this textbook contain professionally written sentences by authors whose works are frequently studied in English classrooms—instead of the artificially concocted sentences in grammar books, written for students to identify grammatical structures rather than to demonstrate the effective use of those structures in good writing.

Most grammar books emphasize identification, not application. SENTENCE COMPOSING emphasizes practicing, not identifying; applying, not memorizing. Even though there is constant practice, monotony is unlikely because the methods are varied. The many practices are crucial to learning and using the sentence composing techniques of professional writers.

SENTENCE COMPOSING teaches sentence structures seldom used by students in their writing, frequently used by professional writers in theirs. The aim is to bridge the gap. The method is to isolate the types of sentence structures associated with professional writing and practice them until they become second-nature.

"Practicing Professional Sentence Composing Techniques, " Part I of the textbook, introduces the four sentence composing techniques used throughout:

SENTENCE SCRAMBLING

SENTENCE IMITATING

SENTENCE COMBINING

SENTENCE EXPANDING

The purpose is to establish an awareness of the variety of sentence structures common in the hundreds of professionally written sentences used for the practices in this textbook. Once that awareness is established, you'll apply it by producing sentences with sentence structures resembling those of professional writers.

"Using Professional Sentence Structures," Part II of the textbook, builds upon the awareness established in Part I and focuses your attention on three important structures that are common in professional sentences: absolutes, appositives, and participles. Using the four sentence composing techniques, you'll have intensive practice in these three important structures that sharply differentiate the writing of professionals from the writing of most students.

"Achieving Professional Sentence Variety," Part III of the textbook, uses those three structures, adds others, and teaches the three positions within a sentence that professional writers use in ways much different from students: sentence openers, S-V splits, and sentence closers. Using the four sentence composing techniques, the practices focus on how professional writers effectively use these three positions.

All of the textbook concentrates on sentence composing skills through the use of model sentences by professional writers. Constant exposure to their sentence structures will produce attention to, understanding of, and, with practice, natural use of such structures by you in your own sentences.

An important purpose of SENTENCE COMPOSING is to provide you with alternatives from which you can make appropriate choices for the sentences you compose. If you're like most students, you're unaware that there are alternatives, and may be puzzled by exactly what is meant by "sentence variety" and "sentence maturity." Choice requires awareness of alternatives. This textbook provides the awareness. It also provides the alternatives necessary to help you improve the way you compose sentences.

The section in the back of the textbook called "References" contains the original sentences by professional writers that were the basis for the practices. They're included so that you'll have immediate feedback on how you did in the individual practices. You should not, however, consider the References "answers in the back of the book." They're for comparison, not correction. The important thing isn't whether your sentence is like the professional writer's, but whether you learn anything from the comparison. You may decide that the professional writer's is better; in that case, study the differences. You may decide that yours is just as good; in that case, congratulate yourself. You may decide that yours is better; in that case, take a bow. In any case, the important thing to remember is that the References are not "answers."

I

Practicing Professional
Sentence Composing Techniques

When you write sentences and when professional writers write sentences, you both engage in a similar process. The results, however, are often different, sometimes dramatically so. The difference isn't spelling, capitalization, or other conventions of written English. It's true that many students have problems with such matters. It is also true that you rarely find mechanical flaws in published writing. Authors are not necessarily better in these respects; they may just have good editors.

A big difference (and the one this textbook deals with) is in sentence structure variety. You'll recognize this difference as you practice "sentence composing"—that is, producing sentences closely resembling in structure those written by professional writers. SENTENCE COMPOSING focuses on sentence structure as a major difference between the sentences of professionals and those of students. The text provides model sentences written by professionals. You'll practice writing your own sentences with structures similar to the ones in the models. The goal is to establish those structures in your own writing.

In this part of the textbook, you'll study four sentence composing techniques that will enable you to write sentences similar in structure to those of professional writers: sentence scrambling, sentence imitating, sentence combining, and sentence expanding. The techniques themselves are easy to learn; however, in order to apply them to your own writing, you must practice them frequently. The book provides numerous practices for that reason. Don't make the mistake of thinking that just because you can do the technique, you'll apply it in your own writing. The application of the skill to your own writing is more likely to occur if you do most of the practices on the particular sentence composing techniques emphasized in each part of the book.

You can learn much about writing in general, not only sentence structure, through the practices in this book. The study of the sentence has too often been neglected as a way of improving writing; instead the

1

study of the sentence was used mainly for analyzing grammar. SENTENCE COMPOSING studies the sentence as a way of improving your writing. Even though you'll be working mostly with sentences, there's much that you can learn about good writing of any length and type—paragraphs, essays, short stories, reports, and research papers.

1

Sentence Scrambling

DEFINING SENTENCE SCRAMBLING

Sentence scrambling simply means mixing up the parts of a sentence and then putting them back together to make a meaningful, well-written sentence. Sentence scrambling permits a close look at how professional writers assemble the parts of their sentences.

The sentence parts are listed in a different order from that in the original sentence. To illustrate, here's an original sentence, a list with the sentence parts in the same order as in the original, and a list with the sentence parts scrambled.

Original Sentence

When his father, who was old and twisted with toil, made over to him the ownership of the farm and seemed content to creep away to a corner and wait for death, he shrugged his shoulders and dismissed the old man from his mind.

Sherwood Anderson, Winesburg, Ohio

Original Order

1. When his father,
2. who was old
3. and twisted with toil,
4. made over to him the ownership
5. of the farm
6. and seemed content
7. to creep away
8. to a corner
9. and wait for death,
10. he shrugged his shoulders
11. and dismissed the old man
12. from his mind.

Scrambled Order

1. to a corner
2. from his mind.
3. and wait for death,
4. When his father,
5. he shrugged his shoulders
6. made over to him the ownership
7. who was old
8. and dismissed the old man
9. of the farm
10. and twisted with toil,
11. to creep away
12. and seemed content

PRACTICING SENTENCE SCRAMBLING

PRACTICE 1

In these two lists of scrambled sentence parts, the content is nonsense, but the structure is grammatically meaningful. The sentence parts are scrambled versions of the model sentence above the lists. Unscramble them to produce a sentence identical in structure to the model. Write out the completed sentences. Compare your sentences with the ones in the References on page 132.

Model

When his father, who was old and twisted with toil, made over to him the ownership of the farm and seemed content to creep away to a corner and wait for death, he shrugged his shoulders and dismissed the old man from his mind.

Sherwood Anderson, Winesburg, Ohio

List One: Nonsense Sentence Parts (in scrambled order)

1. and covered the floor
2. and feathered with grease
3. with its typewriters
4. which was solid
5. when the ashtray
6. sang for him the dance
7. and became encouraged
8. to an ocean
9. the crab blanked its pencil

10. and hope for mud
11. of the petunia
12. to jump up

List Two: Nonsense Sentence Parts (in scrambled order)

1. in an instant
2. which was crystal
3. the bun opened its halves
4. although the hamburger
5. ran down to him the story
6. in a dictionary
7. of the onion
8. and demented in town
9. and seemed reluctant
10. and study for words
11. to fly away
12. and embraced the cheese

PRACTICE 2

For each sentence there are two separate lists of equivalent sentence parts. The two lists, though structurally identical to each other and to the structure of the model sentence, are different in content. The first list is written in sense language; the second, in nonsense. The purpose of the use of nonsense language is to remove as much meaning as possible from the list of sentence parts. Without the possibility of being distracted by the meaning of each of the sentence parts, you can focus on the major aspect of sentence composing, that is, sentence structure. It will be more helpful to you if you write out the unscrambled versions rather than simply list the correct order of the sentence parts. Doing so will give you practice in writing the various sentence structures. Punctuate correctly, following the punctuation used in the model sentence in each case. Compare your sentences with the ones in the References on page 132.

Tom got his lantern, lit it in the hogshead, wrapped it closely in the towel, and the two adventurers crept in the gloom toward the tavern.

Mark Twain, *Tom Sawyer*

1a. ahead of the singer
 b. rehearsed it
 c. Bob wrote his song
 d. but the small orchestra played
 e. sang it beautifully
 f. in the play

g. in the evenings
h. with the beat

2a. and the plimey peesto scrunted
b. broded it
c. in the tunert
d. Snaze kurped its blander
e. crassed it frinkly
f. of a bleepert
g. from the marton
h. with the snart

To carry care to bed is to sleep with a pack on your back.

Thomas Haliburton

3a. in a state
b. to bring work
c. of constant worry
d. is
e. from the office
f. to "relax"

4a. in a zipple
b. to jeld crams
c. is
d. near town
e. from a zapple
f. to murd

The man who writes about himself and his own time is the only man who writes about all people and about all time.

George Bernard Shaw

5a. with great enthusiasm
b. a sportscaster
c. and with solid knowledge
d. the choice announcer
e. is
f. who communicates
g. who communicates
h. and sports' top athletes
i. with fans

6a. and near forty bloops
b. the blends
c. the best blends
d. and their brained nabort

e. which croak
f. are
g. which croak
h. near thirty bleeps
i. from selfhoose

A leather handbag, extremely worn, but with a label inside it as impressive as the one inside Mrs. Snell's hat, lay on the pantry.

J. D. Salinger, "Down at the Dinghy"

7a. very dry
b. in Grandma's eyes
c. as appealing
d. the wrinkled skin
e. as the sparkle
f. shone in the candlelight
g. about it
h. yet with a softness

8a. an oversized saltert
b. in its woostem
c. quite pritert
d. as lumrious
e. plazoned from a yambrod
f. as a klanion
g. on it
h. and of a color

PRACTICE 3

To recognize that sentence parts are movable, do the following Practice. For each list of scrambled sentence parts, unscramble the parts three times, each time producing a sentence with the parts in a different order. Punctuate accordingly. Indicate which of the three versions you consider the most effective arrangement, and explain your choice. Then check the References on page 133 to compare your choices with the sentences as originally written.

EXAMPLE

Scrambled Sentence Parts

a. so coldly burning
b. falling upon his knees
c. which was so huge

d. as he watched the Star

e. he began to pray humbly

Unscrambled Sentences (three versions)

1. Falling upon his knees as he watched the Star, which was so huge, so coldly burning, he began to pray humbly.
2. He began to pray humbly, falling upon his knees, as he watched the Star, which was so huge, so coldly burning.
3. As he watched the Star, which was so huge, so coldly burning, falling upon his knees, he began to pray humbly.

The most effective version is the first. The second is less well organized, with the main actions (praying, falling on his knees) appearing secondary to the description of the Star. The third version places the phrase *falling upon his knees* in a position in which it seems to describe the Star rather than the person.

1a. leaving the oak box of money

b. leaving the quirt

c. he ran from the place

d. leaving his suitcase

John Steinbeck, *East of Eden*

2a. and tight

b. a mortgage financier

c. the father was respectable

d. and forecloser

e. and a stern, upright collection-plate passer

O. Henry, "The Ransom of Red Chief"

3a. for nothing can be done

b. after Buck Fanshaw's inquest

c. without a public meeting

d. a meeting of the short-haired brotherhood was held

e. on the Pacific coast

f. and an expression of sentiment.

Mark Twain. "Buck Fanshaw's Funeral"

4a. the littlest

b. with them

c. I had ever seen

d. carrying a gnarled walking stick

e. oldest man

f. was Elmo Goodhue Pipgrass

Max Shulman, "The Unlucky Winner"

5a. over long woolen underwear
   b. he bounded
   c. around his chest
   d. out of bed
   e. and a leather jacket
   f. wearing a long flannel nightgown
   g. a nightcap

James Thurber, "The Night the Ghost Got In"

6a. looked up from his scrambled eggs
   b. once upon a sunny morning
   c. who sat in a breakfast nook
   d. quietly cropping the roses
   e. with a gold horn
   f. a man
   g. to see a white unicorn
   h. in the garden

James Thurber, "The Unicorn in the Garden"

7a. grabbed my right foot
   b. of patent-leather dancing pumps
   c. then
   d. and shoved it into one of them
   e. as a shoehorn
   f. she removed the gleaming pair
   g. out of a box on the bed
   h. using her finger

Jean Shepherd, "Wanda Hickey's Night of Golden Memories"

PRACTICE 4

Select 20 sentences from several pieces of writing you've done in the past. Choose sentences in which the sentence parts may be repositioned. For each, reposition various sentence parts, trying different arrangements. Write two alternative versions for each sentence in which the only change is the repositioning of the sentence parts. Indicate which of the sentence arrangements you prefer and why.

2

Sentence Imitating

DEFINING SENTENCE IMITATING

Sentence imitating is the use of professional writers' sentences as models for writing your own sentences. The structure of your sentence is the same as the model's, but the content is different. The purpose is to increase your ability to vary sentence structure through a deliberate imitation of the structure of the model sentence.

PRACTICING SENTENCE IMITATING

PRACTICE 1

Below are groups of three sentences. Two of the sentences in each group are identical in structure. The other sentence in the group, although competently written, is structurally different from the other two. Identify the sentence that is different. Answers are in the References on page 133.

    1a. Great was his care of them.
     b. Something else he saw.
     c. Chilling was her story of passion.

    2a. The big thing, exciting yet frightening, was to talk to her, say what he hoped to do.
     b. There was also a rhino, who, from the tracks and the kicked-up mound of strawy dung, came there each night.
     c. An acceptable solution, simple and efficient, is to negotiate with the management, emphasize what the workers want to delete.

    3a. Much later the accountant finished, ledgers in their vertical files on the right side of the desk, pencils and pens in the container decorated with seals and designs on the shelf above the desk.

b. This leader, whose word was law among the boys who defied authority for the sake of defiance, was no more than twelve or thirteen years old and looked even younger.

c. Soon afterwards they retired, Mama in her big oak bed on one side of the room, Emilio and Rosy in their boxes full of straw and sheepskins on the other side of the room.

4a. During rush-hour traffic, when his nerves were frazzled, Brent Hammond, twenty miles above the speed limit, hit his brakes, from which came sharp peals and leaden grindings as though the metal were alive and hurting.

b. On stormy nights, when the tide was out, the bay of Fougere, fifty feet below the house, resembled an immense black pit, from which arose mutterings and sighs as if the sands down there had been alive and complaining.

c. Aleck Sander stood out from the shadows, walking, already quite near in the moonless dark, a little taller than Big Ed, though there was only a few months' difference between them.

5a. Listening to evaluate the difference between the two violins, the concertmaster chose, glancing back and forth over the two instruments, the one with the slightly arched bow.

b. Light flickered on bits of ruby glass and on sensitive capillary hairs in the nylon-brushed nostrils of the creature that quivered gently, gently, its eight legs spidered under it on rubber-padded paws.

c. Pretending to take an interest in the New Season's Models, Gumbril made, squinting sideways over the burning tips of his cigar, an inventory of her features.

6a. He reached over for the submachine gun, took the clip out that was in the magazine, felt in his pockets for the clips, opened the action and looked through the barrel, put the clip back in the groove of the magazine until it clicked, and then looked down the hill slope.

b. Amused yet bewildered, near the sardonic boy in a corner of the cafeteria, with a friend who had invited her and another whose boyfriend was his remarkably opposite twin, Joan thought constantly that noon about the ambivalence of her emotions.

c. Abandoned and helpless, under the crude lean-to in the court-yard of the tin factory, beside the woman who had lost a breast and the man whose burned face was scarcely a face any more, Miss Sasaki suffered awfully that night from the pain in her broken leg.

PRACTICE 2

Compare these two sentences: the first is a model; the second, an imitation. Notice how the imitation relied on the clues (**boldface**) of punctuation and certain kinds of words and word endings.

Model

Pretend**ing to** take an interest in **the** New Season's Models, Gumbril made, squint**ing** sideways **over** the burning tip of his cigar, an inventory of her features.

Aldous Huxley, Antic Hay

Imitation

Listen**ing to** evaluate the difference between **the** two violins, the concertmaster chose, glanc**ing** back and forth **over** the two instruments, the one with the slightly arched bow.

Review the punctuation patterns in the model and the imitation. They are identical. In doing the imitation, the student worked on one sentence part at a time, concentrating on how that particular sentence part is structured, then imitated only that particular sentence part. The process is then repeated with the next sentence part, then the next, the next, and so forth. Using punctuation marks from the model sentence parts, the model has four sentence parts:

First Sentence Part

Model: Pretending to take an interest in the New Season's Models,
Imitation: Listening to evaluate the difference between the two violins,

Second Sentence Part

Model: Gumbril made,
Imitation: the concertmaster chose,

Third Sentence Part

Model: squinting sideways over the burning tip of his cigar,
Imitation: glancing back and forth over the two instruments,

Fourth Sentence Part

Model: an inventory of her features.
Imitation: the one with the slightly arched bow.

Notice that the two sentences are almost identical in structure; however, they are very different in content and somewhat different in length—the imitation uses more words. Duplicating the exact number of words in the model is undesirable. Don't focus on the words; focus, instead, on the structure. Imitate only the structure. You may, however, use some things from the model in your sentence imitation. The use of some of the same words/word endings and the use of the exact punctuation of the model will make sentence imitating easy.

Following the guidelines for sentence imitating mentioned earlier, write an imitation of each of these model sentences.

1. Great was his care of them.

Jack London, All Gold Cañon

2. The big thing, exciting yet frightening, was to talk to her, say what he hoped to do.

Bernard Malamud, The Assistant

3. He had never been hungrier, and he filled his mouth with wine, faintly tarry-tasting from the leather bag, and swallowed.

Ernest Hemingway, For Whom the Bell Tolls

4. Soon afterwards they retired, Mama in her big oak bed on one side of the room, Emilio and Rosy in their boxes full of straw and sheepskins on the other side of the room.

John Steinbeck, "Flight"

5. On stormy nights, when the tide was out, the bay of Fougere, fifty feet below the house, resembled an immense black pit, from which arose mutterings and sighs as if the sands down there had been alive and complaining.

Joseph Conrad, "The Idiots"

To help you, here are sentences imitating the structures of the five model sentences above. The structure words/word endings and punctuation that have been retained from the original sentences are in **boldface** type.

1. Chilling **was her** story **of** passion.
2. An acceptable solution, simple and efficient, is **to** negotiate **with** the management, emphasize **what** the workers want to delete.
3. The horse had never been nast**ier,** and it threw its riders to the ground, cold and hard from the frost, and bolted.
4. Much later the accountant finish**ed,** ledgers **in** their vertical files **on** the right side **of the** desk, pencils and pens **in their** containers decorated with seals **and** designs **on the** shelf **above** the desk.

5. During rush-hour traffic, **when** his nerves were frazzled, Brent Hammond, twenty miles above **the** speed limit, hit his brakes, **from which** came sharp peals and leaden grindings **as** though the metal were alive **and** hurting.

Compare #2 in the imitations with its model. In the model, two words with *ing* suffixes (*exciting* yet *frightening*) modify the subject of the sentence. The imitation uses two adjectives to modify the subject (*simple* and *efficient*). This kind of substitution is often desirable, for it allows more freedom in word choice.

Compare #3 with its model. In the model, one adjective is used at the beginning of this phrase: "faintly *tarry-tasting* from the leather bag." The imitation uses two adjectives at the beginning of the equivalent phrase: "*cold* and *hard* from the frost." Adding structures to those present in the model allows greater flexibility. For example, if the model has one prepositional phrase, you may want to add another one in your imitation; or if a noun is unmodified in the model, you may want to modify it in your imitation.

PRACTICE 3

In order to imitate the structures of professionally written sentences, you must first be able to recognize the structural characteristics of the sentence parts contained within the sentence to be imitated. To do this, read the model sentence several times, sentence part by sentence part, noticing the structure words used and the pattern of punctuation.

From the two sentences (a and b) following each model sentence, select the one that approximates the sentence structure of the model; then write a sentence imitation of the model. All models are from *The Martian Chronicles* by Ray Bradbury.

1. One minute it was Ohio winter, with doors closed, windows locked, the panes blind with frost, icicles fringing every roof, children skiing on slopes, housewives lumbering like great black bears in their furs along the icy streets.

a. Near the race track where the Derby was held, a peanut vendor, with wrinkled skin, a face like an eagle, boldly stood almost directly in the line of the huge traffic, hawking his peanuts, describing their superb taste, rich aroma.

b. Yesterday it was the Boston Marathon, with crowds gathered, police ready, the runners covered with suntan oils, many limbering up, even wheelchair participants checking their equipment like careful auto mechanics with their tools of all sorts.

2. Named but unnamed and borrowing from humans everything but humanity, the robots stared at the nailed lids of their labeled

F.O.B. boxes, in a death that was not even a death, for there had never been a life.

a. With the carousel slide projector carefully placed atop several books to provide the right height for perfect screen projection, with the slides placed within it, the right organization for the presentation, the lesson began.

b. Hesitant but not uncertain, and drawing from libraries all of her knowledge, she walked into the room for her comprehensive examination, with a feeling that was certainly not calm, because there would always be the unknown.

3. Here and there a fire, forgotten in the last rush, lingered and in a sudden access of strength fed upon the dry bones of some littered shack.

a. Once or twice the siren, obscured by the sudden explosion, echoed but with a dreadful parody of itself sounded with a noise like a banshee.

b. Now and then, he tweaked his painted, bulbous nose, and the children nearby giggled at the bicycle-horn sound.

PRACTICE 4

Write an imitation of each of the model sentences below.

1. One of these dogs, the best one, had disappeared.

Fred Gipson, *Old Yeller*

2. Among the company was a lawyer, a young man of about twenty-five.

Anton Chekhov, "The Bet"

3. Halfway there he heard the sound he dreaded, the hollow, rasping cough of a horse.

John Steinbeck, *The Red Pony*

4. Poppa, a good quiet man, spent the last hours before our parting moving aimlessly about the yard, keeping to himself and avoiding me.

Gordon Parks, "My Mother's Dream for Me"

5. Standing in the truck bed, holding onto the bars of the sides, rode the others, twelve-year-old Ruthie and ten-year-old Winfield, grime-faced and wild, their eyes tired but excited, their fingers and the edges of their mouths black and sticky from licorice whips, whined out of their father in town.

John Steinbeck, *The Grapes of Wrath*

PRACTICE 5

For each of the four model sentences below, there are two sentence imitations. Each of the sentence imitations approximates the structure of the model. Do three things. First, match the imitations for each model. Next, indicate which words/word endings have been retained in the limitations (these are the structure words/word endings that gave the writers of the imitation clues to the structure). Finally, write an imitation of each model.

Models

1. Near the spot upriver to which Mr. Tanimoto had transported the priests, there sat a large case of rice cakes which a rescue party had evidently brought for the wounded lying thereabouts but hadn't distributed.

John Hersey, Hiroshima

2. There was also a rhino, who, from the tracks and the kicked-up mound of strawy dung, came there each night.

Ernest Hemingway, Green Hills of Africa

3. The dark silence was there and the heavy shapes, sitting, and the little blue light burning.

Ray Bradbury, The Vintage Bradbury

4. Light flickered on bits of ruby glass and on sensitive capillary hairs in the nylon-brushed nostrils of the creature that quivered gently, gently, its eight legs spidered under it on rubber-padded paws.

Ray Bradbury, Fahrenheit 451

Imitations

a. Stars twinkled on pieces of broken shells and on ruined sand castles in the sea-drenched sand of the beach that stretched miles, endless miles, its many shells strewn on it by high-crested waves.

b. At the place in the room where he had left his books, there was a stack of journals that had evidently been brought by several of the more academic students but hadn't been used by the teacher.

c. The dense fog was there and the bloody bodies, dying, and the torn white flag waving.

d. I sat on velvet grass and under spreading blue leaves in the light-yellow atmosphere of a planet that orbited, slowly, steadily, its six moons clinging close like new-born children.

e. There was also a turtle, who, from the half-eaten tomato and the hole under the fence, had visited the garden that day.

f. The big race was ready to begin and the line of cars, waiting, and the red flag still standing.

g. There was also the horror, which, from the odor and snake-belly sensation of dead flesh, came there each time.

h. Outside the shack from which the patrol had started shooting, there was a blast of gunfire that the rebels had intended for the door lock but hadn't hit.

PRACTICE 6

Here are six paragraphs, all with the same number of sentences (five). Three are student imitations of Lindbergh's paragraph. Identify these three.

Model Paragraph

1. This is a snail shell, round, full, and glossy as a horse chestnut. 2. Comfortable and compact, it sits curled up like a cat in the hollow of my hand. 3. Milky and opaque, it has the pinkish bloom of the sky on a summer evening, ripening to rain. 4. On its smooth, symmetrical face is pencilled with precision a perfect spiral, winding inward to the pin point center of the shell, the tiny dark core of the apex, the pupil of the eye. 5. It stares at me, this mysterious single eye—and I stare back.

Anne Morrow Lindbergh, *Gift from the Sea*

Paragraph One

1. The school bus pulled up and let the children out. 2. One of the little boys was running after his dog. 3. The dog had followed him to school and refused to go home when the boy chased him. 4. The other students thought it was funny when the dog ran into the school building. 5. Somebody had left the door open on purpose.

Paragraph Two

1. When it snowed yesterday, I was at the library. 2. The library is one near where I live and has many books that can help a lot with the assignments from school. 3. A lot of my friends go there to visit with each other and to do some research and studying. 4. The librarians are helpful when you need to find some book to do a history or English assignment. 5. I like the library!

Paragraph Three

1. There is a snowflake, light, delicate, and fluffy as a piece of

cotton. 2. Swirling and blowing, it floats down from the sky like the seeds of the milkweed plant. 3. White and bright, it has the gleam of the blinding sunlight and the reflecting moonlight, shining in silver. 4. On its surface is stenciled a star, formed with its five or six symmetrical points, the arms of the snowflake, the body of it. 5. It falls to earth, this crystal of beauty—and the earth melts it.

Paragraph Four

1. This is an old book, interesting, long, but thought-provoking as a philosophical treatise. 2. Soiled but well read, it remains standing upright on my bookshelf mixed in with paperbacks. 3. Analytic and probing, it reveals many pitfalls in the process of thinking, describing wrong conclusions. 4. In its yellow pages are recorded with skill many criticisms, converging ultimately into the story of all people, the universal, timeless tale of every individual, the discourse on humanity. 5. It speaks of man, this lengthy discourse—yet man ignores it.

Paragraph Five

1. Some rock stars are very colorful and exciting to watch when they perform at a live concert. 2. Usually hundreds or thousands of teenagers attend these concerts, which are usually held in large convention halls or sometimes outdoors in large parks or other public places. 3. Music-lovers look forward to attending these exciting events. 4. Despite what many people say, the behavior at the concerts is very good. 5. It is noisy, but since noise is what anyone would expect at such concerts, nobody there really minds.

Paragraph Six

1. This is a room, dark, comfortable, and at times lonely as a silent cave. 2. Small and private, it can absorb my thoughts like a sponge. 3. Comfortable and secure, the room has a feeling of safety and peace, providing a hiding place. 4. On its walls are varicolored posters, all reflecting moods of mine, ranging from joy to despair. 5. The posters face me, those mirrors of my soul—and I reminisce.

PRACTICE 7

Write a five-sentence descriptive paragraph. Model your sentence structures after those of Lindbergh's description of the snail shell. You may choose anything to describe—a writing instrument, an old family picture, a pet, a sports player in action. Or, use one of the four starter sentences below. If you choose one of these sentences, use it as your first sentence of the paragraph.

1. This is an attic, musty, dark, and forbidding as London fog.
2. This is an eye, glassy, bloodshot, and unfocused as a bad camera shot.
3. This is a crystal goblet, sparkling, clear, and dazzling as a diamond.
4. Here is a baby, soft, warm, and pink as a rose.

Remember that in sentence imitating it's not necessary to duplicate the sentence structure of the model exactly. Notice in the imitation sentences above that some add structures that were not in the model, some make changes in the structure, and some drop structures that were in the model. All of the imitations are, however, enough like the model in sentence structure to be acceptable sentence imitations.

PRACTICE 8

Write an original paragraph five to 10 sentences in length. Include somewhere in the paragraph a sentence imitation of as many of the following model sentences as you can. Even if you use only one or two model sentences for imitation, in the rest of your paragraph try to write sentences (without the use of models) that are similar in structure to those associated with professional writing.

1. Over this rocky area relieved by a few shady tall persimmon trees the graduating class walked.

    Maya Angelou, *I Know Why the Caged Bird Sings*

2. A few hours before, he adored me, was devoted and worshipful, and now he was angry.

    Anaïs Nin, *The Diary of Anaïs Nin*

3. Behind a billboard, on an empty lot, he opened the purse and saw a pile of silver and copper coins.

    Charles Spencer Chaplin (Charlie Chaplin), *My Autobiography*

4. The frozen earth thawed, leaving the short grass looking wet and weary.

    Peter Abraham, *Tell Freedom*

5. I was fourteen at the time, too young for a full-time job, but I managed to get a Bronx Home News route, for which I paid five dollars a week.

    Milton Kaplan, *Commentary*

6. In my robe and barefoot in the backyard, under cover of going to see about my new beans, I gave myself up to the gentle warmth and thanked God that no matter what evil I had done in my life He had allowed me to live to see this day.

    Maya Angelou, *I Know Why the Caged Bird Sings*

7. Certainly no one was strong enough to control them, least of all their mother, the queen-bee of the hive, on whom nine-tenths of the burden fell, on whose strength they all depended, but whose children were much too self-willed and self-confident to take guidance from her, or from any one else, unless in the direction they fancied.

Henry Adams, The Education of Henry Adams

Sentence imitating is certainly not an end in itself. The goal of sentence imitating is to allow you to become familiar with the structural possibilities for composing sentences through careful attention to the ways in which professional writers structure their sentences. The variety of sentence structure possibilities is endless. In this section of the book only a small portion of those possibilities has been shown. Through the practices you should have become aware of those possibilities. This awareness is crucial to the ultimate goal of sentence imitating: writing sentences structured in mature, varied ways, similar to those of professional writers, but *without* the use of model sentences. In other words, sentence imitating is designed to provide a means for your independent use of sentence structure variety in your own writing. Having learned what sentence structure variety is possible, you can now apply this knowledge in your own writing.

3

Sentence Combining

DEFINING SENTENCE COMBINING

Sentence combining is the process of integrating two or more related sentences into one sentence. Unlike sentence scrambling and sentence imitating, in which you were given the structure for the sentence parts, sentence combining provides only the content. You provide the sentence structure in which to express that content, thereby contributing one-half of the resulting sentence.

Sentence Combining Through Inserting

This process is quite common in this section on sentence combining and is frequently done with inserts from several sentences combined into one sentence.

Multi-Sentence Version: He paused. He was puffing noisily.
Single-Sentence Version: He paused, puffing noisily.

John Steinbeck, *The Red Pony*

Multi-Sentence Version: His head was aching. His throat was sore. He forgot to light his cigarette.
Single-Sentence Version: His head aching, his throat sore, he forgot to light his cigarette.

Sinclair Lewis, *Cass Timberlane*

Multi-Sentence Version: Bernard was waiting outside. He was waiting on the landing. He was wearing three things. One was a sweater. It was a turtleneck. It was black. Another was flannels. They were dirty. The third thing was slippers.
Single-Sentence Version: Bernard, wearing a black turtleneck sweater, dirty flannels, and slippers, was waiting on the landing outside.

Brian Moore, *The Lonely Passion of Judith Hearne*

21

Sentence Combining Through Changing

Unlike the previous examples in which no words were changed but some were dropped, in the next examples words are changed as well as dropped. The changes involve either a substitution of one word for another or a change in the grammatical form of the same word. The changes are usually slight, but they are necessary to ensure that the resulting sentence, from two or more sentences, is smooth and grammatically correct.

> *Multi-Sentence Version:* Their cabins looked neat and snug. This occurred in the frosty December dusk. Their cabins had pale blue smoke. The smoke rose from the chimneys and doorways. The chimneys and doorways glowed amber from the fires inside.
> *Single-Sentence Version:* In the frosty December dusk, their cabins looked neat and snug with pale blue smoke rising from the chimneys and doorways glowing amber from the fires inside.
>
> Harper Lee, *To Kill a Mockingbird*

In this example, one of the words (*had*) is changed to a different word in the single-sentence version (*with*). Two of the words (*rose, glowed*) are changed to different grammatical forms of the same words in the single-sentence version (*rising, glowing*). The changes provide smoothness and grammatical correctness in the single-sentence version.

PRACTICING SENTENCE COMBINING

PRACTICE 1

Before you practice combining sentences, try the reverse: de-combining sentences. De-combining professionally written sentences provides much insight into the writing process. It rarely matters whether the original sentence is short, medium, or long. Here are three professionally written sentences, one of each length, with the lists of sentences resulting from sentence de-combining:

Sentence De-Combining: Short Sentence

Silently, desperately, he fought with all his weapons.

Katherine Anne Porter, *Ship of Fools*

1. He fought.
2. The fighting was with weapons.
3. The weapons were his.
4. All of his weapons were used.
5. The fighting was done silently.
6. The fighting was done desperately.

Sentence De-Combining: Medium Sentence

Once his back happened to be half turned toward the door, and, hearing a noise there, he wheeled and sprang up, uttering a loud cry.

Stephen Crane, "The Blue Hotel"

1. Once something happened.
2. What happened was that his back happened to be half turned.
3. His back was half turned toward the door.
4. During this time he heard a noise there.
5. Upon hearing it, he wheeled.
6. Upon hearing it, he sprang up.
7. During the wheeling and the springing up, he was doing something.
8. He was uttering a loud cry.

Sentence De-Combining: Long Sentence

He backed Jack up against the ropes, measured him and then hooked the left very light to the side of Jack's head and socked the right into the body as hard as he could sock, just as low as he could get it.

Ernest Hemingway, "Fifty Grand"

1. He backed Jack up.
2. The backing was against the ropes.
3. He measured him.
4. Then he hooked the left.
5. The hook was very light.
6. The hook was to the side of the head.
7. The head was Jack's.
8. He socked the right.
9. He socked it into the body.
10. The socking was as hard as he could sock.
11. The socking was as low as he could get it.

Study the three examples of sentence de-combining above. Notice how several of the sentences in the list were derived from one sentence part of the author's sentence, how the next group was derived from the next sentence part of the author's sentence, and so forth. The purpose of this Practice is to focus on how a skillful writer packs a lot into one sentence.

In this Practice, de-combine each of the sentences below, one sentence part at a time, to produce two or more sentences for each sentence part in the original. The number of sentences you can list is not fixed. Try for more rather than fewer sentences. In doing so, you'll become more conscious of the greater economy, variety, and therefore maturity of the original sentence.

1. The fixer got up on his raw hands and bleeding knees and went on, blindly crawling across the yard.

Bernard Malamud, *The Fixer*

2. She flicked her wrist neatly out of Doctor Harry's pudgy careful fingers and pulled the sheet up to her chin.

Katherine Anne Porter, "The Jilting of Granny Weatherall"

3. On the table, covered with oilcloth figured with clusters of blue grapes, a place was set, and he smelled hot coffee-cake of some kind.

Willa Cather, "Neighbor Rosicky"

4. Every old woman was a doctor, and gathered her own medicines in the woods, and knew how to compound doses that would stir the vitals of a cast-iron dog.

Mark Twain, *Mark Twain's Autobiography*

5. She cleared away the smoking things, then drew back the cotton bedspread from the bed she had been sitting on, took off her slippers, and got into bed.

J. D. Salinger, *Franny and Zooey*

6. The driver of the car stopped it, slamming it to a skidding halt on the greasy pavement without warning, actually flinging the two passengers forward until they caught themselves with their braced hands against the dash.

William Faulkner, "Delta Autumn"

PRACTICE 2

Each of the lists of sentences below was derived from a single sentence written by a professional writer. Your task is to combine all of the sentences into just one sentence, following the order of the list. Punctuate correctly. After you complete each one, compare your sentence with the original in the References on page 134.

1a. The boy watched.
  b. During the watching, his eyes did something.
  c. His eyes were bulging.
  d. All of this occurred in the dark.

Based on a sentence by Edmund Ware, "An Underground Episode"

2a. One of the dogs had done something.
  b. This dog was the best one of all the dogs.
  c. It had disappeared.

Based on a sentence by Fred Gipson, *Old Yeller*

3a. Doctor Parcival was jumping to his feet.
 b. At the same time he was breaking off the tale.
 c. Doctor Parcival began to walk up and down.
 d. The office in which he walked was of the *Winesburg Eagle*.
 e. In that office someone sat.
 f. The someone was George Willard.
 g. As George sat, he was listening.

Based on a sentence by Sherwood Anderson, Winesburg, Ohio

4a. This land was waterless.
 b. It was furred with cacti.
 c. The cacti could store water.
 d. In addition, the land was furred with the great-rooted brush.
 e. The brush could reach deep into the earth.
 f. The brush would do this to get a little moisture.
 g. The brush could get along on very little moisture.

Based on a sentence by John Steinbeck, The Pearl

5a. It glided through.
 b. As it glided, it brushed the twigs.
 c. The twigs were overhanging.
 d. It disappeared from the river.
 e. It disappeared like some creature.
 f. The creature was slim.
 g. The creature was amphibious.
 h. The creature was leaving the water.
 i. The creature was going for its lair.
 j. The lair was in the forests.

Based on a sentence by Joseph Conrad, "The Lagoon"

PRACTICE 3

Combine each list of sentences twice to produce two different versions. The purpose is variety of expression. Punctuate correctly. Indicate which of the two is more effective, and briefly explain the reasons for your choice.

In this Practice you needn't necessarily stick to the order of ideas in the list. You may use any arrangement you think will produce a good sentence. Compare your best sentences with the authors' in the References on page 135. Which are better? Why?

1a. The house was most enjoyable.
 b. The house was in the country.
 c. The enjoyment of the house was on a particular afternoon.
 d. The afternoon was wintry.

Based on a sentence by James Thurber, "The Owl in the Attic"

2a. The earth was bloody in the setting light.
  b. The bloodiness was caused by the sun.
  c. The sun was setting.
  d. At the same time, the truck came back.

Based on a sentence by John Steinbeck, The Grapes of Wrath

3a. He moves nervously.
  b. He moves fast.
  c. His movement, however, has a restraint.
  d. The restraint suggests that he is a cautious man.
  e. The restraint suggests that he is a thoughtful man.

Based on a sentence by John Hersey, Hiroshima

4a. The girls stood aside.
  b. The very small children rolled in the dust.
  c. Some children clung to the hands of their older brothers or sisters.
  d. The girls were doing two things.
  e. They looked over their shoulders at the boys.
  f. They talked among themselves.

Based on a sentence by Shirley Jackson, "The Lottery"

5a. The cake was shaped in a frying pan.
  b. He took flour.
  c. He took oil.
  d. He shaped them into a cake.
  e. The stove functioned on gas.
  f. The gas was bottled.
  g. He lighted the stove.
  h. The stove was little.

Based on a sentence by Albert Camus, "The Guest"

PRACTICE 4

In this Practice, combine the sentences in the lists using the fewest possible words. The purpose is economy of expression. The number of words in the author's sentence is indicated. Don't worry about using that exact number, but try not to exceed it by much. Compare your sentences with the originals in the References on page 135.

1a. He distributed handbills for merchants.
  b. He did this, and the following activities, from ages ten to fifteen.
  c. He held horses.
  d. He ran confidential errands.
  Word Count: 15

Based on a sentence by Thornton Wilder, The Bridge of San Luis Rey

2a. Nick looked down into the water.
  b. The water was clear.
  c. The water was brown.
  d. The brown color came from the pebbly bottom.
  e. As Nick looked down he watched the trout.
  f. The trout were keeping themselves steady in the current.
  g. They kept themselves steady with their fins.
  h. Their fins were wavering.
   Word Count: 25

Based on a sentence by Ernest Hemingway, "Big Two-Hearted River"

3a. On one side was a tiny meadow.
  b. The meadow began at the very lip of the pool.
  c. The meadow had a surface of green.
  d. The surface was cool.
  e. The surface was resilient.
  f. The surface extended.
  g. The surface extended to the base.
  h. The base was of the browning wall.
   Word Count: 30

Based on a sentence by Jack London, "All-Gold Cañon"

4a. In the stillness of the air many things in the forest seemed to have been bewitched.
  b. They were bewitched into an immobility.
  c. The immobility was perfect.
  d. The immobility was final.
  e. Every tree seemed thus bewitched.
  f. Every leaf seemed thus bewitched.
  g. Every bough seemed thus bewitched.
  h. Every tendril of creeper seemed thus bewitched.
  i. Every petal of minute blossoms seemed thus bewitched.
   Word Count: 33

Based on a sentence by Joseph Conrad, "The Lagoon"

PRACTICE 5

In this Practice, you create paragraphs because the sentences are related in content. As a general guideline, the number of words contained in the original sentence is indicated. You shouldn't necessarily aim for exact duplication of this number. Instead, try to approximate it. Try for clear meaning, word economy, and sentence variety. Compare your results with the originals in the References on page 135. If the authors' sentences are better, note the reasons.

Paragraph One

Narration of a bull fight from "The Undefeated" by Ernest Hemingway (five sentences):

1a. Manuel waved his hand.
   b. Manuel was leaning against the barrera.
   c. Manuel was watching the bull.
   d. And the gypsy ran out.
   e. The gypsy was trailing his cape.
   Word Count: 19 (medium sentence)

2a. The bull pivoted.
   b. The bull was in full gallop.
   c. And the bull charged the cape.
   d. The bull's head was down.
   e. The bull's tail was rising.
   Word Count: 16 (medium sentence)

3a. The gypsy moved.
   b. The movement was in a zigzag.
   c. And as he passed, the bull caught sight of him.
   d. The bull abandoned the cape.
   e. The reason for the abandonment was to charge the man.
   Word Count: 24 (medium sentence)

4a. The gypsy sprinted and vaulted the red fence.
   b. The red fence was of the barrera.
   c. As the gypsy sprinted and vaulted, the bull struck something.
   d. The bull struck the red fence of the barrera.
   e. The bull struck it with his horns.
   Word Count: 19 (medium sentence)

5a. He tossed into it with his horns.
   b. He tossed into it twice.
   c. He was banging into the wood.
   d. He was banging blindly.
   Word Count: 13 (short sentence)

Paragraph Two

Description and explanation of a native african bushman dance from *The Harmless People* by Elizabeth Marshall Thomas (four sentences):

1a. To have a dance the women do certain things.
   b. They sit in a circle.
   c. Their babies are on their backs.
   d. Their babies are asleep.

e. The women sing medicine songs.
f. The songs are sung in several parts.
g. The songs are sung in falsetto voices.
h. During the singing the women clap their hands.
i. The clapping is done in rhythm.
j. The rhythm is sharp.
k. The rhythm is staccato.
l. The rhythm is at counterpoint to the rhythm of their voices.
   Word Count: 43 (long sentence)

2a. The men dance behind their backs.
 b. The men dance one behind the other.
 c. The men circle slowly around.
 d. The men take steps.
 e. The steps are very short.
 f. The steps are pounding.
 g. The steps are at counterpoint to the rhthyms.
 h. One of the rhythms is the rhythm of the singing.
 i. The other rhythm is the rhythm of the clapping.
    Word Count: 33 (long sentence)

3a. Now and then the men do two things.
 b. They, too, sing.
 c. They sing in their deeper voices.
 d. Another thing they do is use their dance rattles.
 e. Their rattles are made from dry cocoons.
 f. The cocoons are strung together with sinew cords.
 g. Their dance rattles are tied to their legs.
 h. Their dance rattles add a sharp, high clatter.
 i. The high clatter is like the sound of shaken gourds.
 j. The rattling sound is very well timed.
 k. The timing is the result of the men's accurate steps.
    Word Count: 49 (long sentence)

4a. A Bushman dance is a pattern.
 b. The pattern is infinitely complicated.
 c. The pattern consists of two things.
 d. One thing is of voices.
 e. The other thing is of rhythm.
 f. The pattern is an orchestra of bodies.
 g. The pattern makes music that has two characteristics.
 h. One characteristic is that the music is infinitely varied.
 i. The other characteristic is that the music is always precise.
    Word Count: 25 (medium sentence)

PRACTICE 6

In the last Practice, the sentence breaks were indicated; here, however, they aren't. For each paragraph:

1. Decide how many sentences to combine into just one sentence. Do this by combining all sentences that have related content and arranging the content in the best order within your sentence.
2. Avoid monotony. Aim for variety in sentence structure. Vary the sentence lengths (short, medium, and long) as well as the sentence structures.
3. Compare your finished paragraph with those of other students and with the author's original paragraph.

The number of words and sentences contained in the author's paragraph is indicated. It's unnecessary to duplicate that number. Use it as a rough guideline. You need not stick to the order of the content in the list of sentences. Use any order that is smooth and logical. Compare your paragraphs with the originals in the References on page 136.

Paragraph One

Description of a Victorian house from *The Martian Chronicles* by Ray Bradbury. (The author's paragraph has 92 words and four sentences.)

1. An iron deer stood.
2. It stood outside.
3. It stood upon this lawn.
4. A Victorian house stood further up on the green.
5. The house was tall.
6. The house was brown.
7. The house was quiet in the sunlight.
8. The house was all covered with scrolls and rococo.
9. The house's windows were made of blue colored glass.
10. The house's windows were made of pink colored glass.
11. The house's windows were made of yellow colored glass.
12. The house's windows were made of green colored glass.
13. Two things were upon the porch.
14. One was geraniums.
15. The geraniums were hairy.
16. The other was a swing.
17. The swing was old.
18. The swing was hooked into the porch ceiling.
19. The swing now swung back and forth, back and forth.

20. The swinging occurred in a little breeze.
21. A cupola was at the summit of the house.
22. The cupola had diamond leaded-glass windows.
23. The cupola had a dunce-cap roof!

Paragraph Two

A scene at dusk from *Winesburg, Ohio* by Sherwood Anderson. (The author's paragraph has 134 words and five sentences.)

1. A man walked up and down.
2. He was little.
3. He was fat.
4. He walked nervously.
5. He walked upon the veranda.
6. The veranda was half decayed.
7. The veranda was of a small frame house.
8. The house stood near the edge of a ravine.
9. The ravine was near the town of Winesburg, Ohio.
10. The man could see the public highway.
11. He could see the highway across a long field.
12. The field had been seeded for clover.
13. The field, however, had produced only a dense crop of weeds.
14. The weeds were yellow mustard weeds.
15. A wagon went along the public highway.
16. The wagon was filled with berry pickers.
17. The berry pickers were returning from the fields.
18. The berry pickers were youths.
19. The berry pickers were maidens.
20. The berry pickers laughed.
21. The berry pickers shouted.
22. The shouting was boisterous.
23. A boy leaped from the wagon.
24. The boy was clad in a shirt.
25. The shirt was blue.
26. The boy attempted to drag after him one of the maidens.
27. The maiden screamed.
28. The maiden protested.
29. She protested shrilly.
30. The feet of the boy in the road kicked up a cloud.
31. The cloud was of dust.
32. The dust cloud floated across the face of the sun.
33. The sun was departing.

PRACTICE 7

Select two paragraphs, each at least 10 sentences in length, from a piece of writing you've recently done. The paragraphs may be from the same piece of writing or from two different ones. For each paragraph, using sentence combining, reduce the 10 sentences to seven or fewer. In the revised sentences, aim for variety of sentence structure and sentence length.

4

Sentence Expanding

DEFINING SENTENCE EXPANDING

Sentence expanding is a process for changing your sentences into sentences like those of professional writers. It transforms reduced sentences into fully developed sentences.

Reduced Sentence

There stood two squat old-fashioned decanters of cut glass.

Expanded Sentence

In the centre of the table there stood, as sentries to a fruit-stand which upheld a pyramid of oranges and American apples, two squat old-fashioned decanters of cut glass, one containing port and the other dark sherry.

James Joyce, "The Dead"

Sentence expanding improves both content and structure. Joyce could have written the same content in more than one sentence. Compare this version, a rewrite of the original, with Joyce's original sentence:

Two squat old-fashioned decanters stood there. They were in the centre of the table. They were like sentries to a fruit-stand near them. The fruit-stand upheld a pyramid of oranges and American apples. One of the decanters contained port. The other one contained sherry.

The rewrite is poorer than the original one-sentence version for several reasons. It's uneconomical, using six sentences to express what Joyce did in just one sentence; it uses 47 words to Joyce's 39. It's poorly organized, failing to show as clearly as Joyce's the interrelationships among the various objects described. It's uninteresting, beginning each of the six sentences in the same monotonous way, with the subject immediately followed by a verb.

Length, by itself, does not determine whether a sentence is effective. A long sentence can be ineffective; a short one, effective; and vice-versa. Don't think that professional writers use only long, highly expanded sentences. They don't. What characterizes their sentences is the skillful interaction among the sentences in their paragraphs—some short, some medium, others long, some expanded, and the rest unexpanded. Yet, regardless of length or degree of expansion, they are all effective.

PRACTICING SENTENCE EXPANDING

In order to use sentence expanding in your own writing, you must be aware of the expansion possibilities in any sentence—possibilities for "telling more" about the people, places, things, manners, actions, incidents, opinions, explanations, and descriptions mentioned.

Are there any limits to sentence expanding? Is there a point where an expanded sentence, like a balloon filled to over-capacity, could "burst"? As long as a sentence is clear in meaning, it's not over-expanded, regardless of how many words are in the sentence, regardless of how many different structures are present, regardless of how many ideas are packed into it. Among American writers, William Faulkner is famous for the ultralong sentences that characterize his style. The French writer Victor Hugo is often cited as having written one of the longest sentences ever, one that has hundreds of words, in *Les Misérables*. The Irish writer James Joyce went even further, ending his novel *Ulysses* with a sentence that runs over twenty pages!

Even among professional writers, however, such ultralong sentences are rare. Still, on the average, sentences by professional writers are longer than those by students. Sentence expanding practice will make you more aware of the potential for revising your sentences so that they're more like those of the experts.

PRACTICE 1

Compare the reduced sentence and the expanded sentence in each pair, noting the quantity, position, and length of each expression. Write an imitation retaining the complete reduced sentence (content and structure) but retaining only the *structure* of the expansions that were added while providing new content. The new content should blend in smoothly.

EXAMPLE

Reduced Sentence

There stood two squat old-fashioned decanters of cut glass.

Expanded Sentence

In the centre of the table **there stood,** as sentries to a fruit-stand which upheld a pyramid of oranges and American apples, **two squat old-fashioned decanters of cut glass,** one containing port and the other dark sherry.

James Joyce, "The Dead"

Imitation

On a shelf in the china closet **there stood,** like fragile sculptures which boasted an old age and genteel birth, **two squat old-fashioned decanters of cut glass,** one opened, the other un-opened.

1a. Her face was still before him.

   b. Now, in the morning air, her face was still before him.

Edith Wharton, *Ethan Frome*

2a. Al was out already.

   b. Al was out already, **unscrewing the steaming radiator cap with the tips of his fingers, jerking his hand away to escape the spurt when the cap should come loose.**

John Steinbeck, *The Grapes of Wrath*

3a. With them was Elmo Goodhue Pipgrass.

   b. With them, **carrying a gnarled walking stick,** was Elmo Goodhue Pipgrass, **the littlest, oldest man I had ever seen.**

Max Shulman, "The Unlucky Winner"

4a. I chewed thoughtfully on a peanut-butter-and-jelly sandwich, while my mother droned on monotonously.

   b. Later that night, hunched over the kitchen table, still somewhat numbed by the unexpected turn of events, I chewed thoughtfully on a peanut-butter-and-jelly sandwich, while my mother, **hanging over the sink in her rump-sprung Chinese-red chenille bathrobe,** droned on monotonously....

Jean Shepherd, "Wanda Hickey's Night of Golden Memories"

PRACTICE 2

A slash mark indicates a place where the professional writer expanded the reduced sentence. The number indicates how many words were used in each expansion. Expand each reduced sentence in the place indicated by the slash mark (/), using approximately the same number of words. Compare yours with the authors' in the References on page 136.

Reduced Sentence

1. She sprang dynamically to her feet, /3, then swiftly and noise-lessly crossed over to her bed and, /3, dragged out her suitcase.

F. Scott Fitzgerald, "Bernice Bobs Her Hair"

2. He stood there, /4, and Rainsford, /6, heard the general's mocking laugh ring through the jungle.

Richard Connell, "The Most Dangerous Game"

3. /4, he knocked the big man down, and the big man came again, /9.

Maurice Walsh, "The Quiet Man"

4. We spent several evenings together, and the last one was the funniest, /15.

Bennett Cerf, At Random

5. That night in the south upstairs chamber, /18, Emmett lay in a kind of trance.

Jessamyn West, "A Time of Learning"

6. /21, Paul dressed and dashed whistling down the corridor to the elevator.

Willa Cather, "Paul's Case"

PRACTICE 3

In the last Practice, you were given complete sentences to expand. Now try expanding sentence parts and compare your expansions with those in the References on page 137.

The slash marks indicate the places for expansions. The number shows how many words were used by the professional writer, but do not be restricted by it. Use it only as a general guideline for the length of the expansion.

Sentence Parts

1. On the outskirts of town, /5, though at first she did not realize it.

Elizabeth Enright, "Nancy"

2. /6, sweet, hot, and warming in his empty stomach.

Ernest Hemingway, "The Undefeated"

3. When the hostess saw that I was awake and that my safety belt was already fastened, /9, waking the other passengers and asking them to fasten their safety belts.

Robert Bingham, "The Unpopular Passenger"

4. Running up the street with all his might, /11.

Murray Heyert, "The New Kid"

5. Placing a cigarette between his lips, /13.

Liam O'Flaherty, "The Sniper"

6. At night, untired after the day's work, /14.

Jessamyn West, "A Time of Learning"

PRACTICE 4

In this practice, you decide the length and position of each expansion. For the first four sentences, add one expansion. Compare yours with the originals in the References on page 137. (The original sentences have just one expansion.) For the next four sentences, add two expansions. Compare yours with the originals in the References on page 138. (The original sentences have two expansions.) Punctuate correctly.

Add One Expansion

1. In the hall stood an enormous trunk.

Willa Cather, *Youth and the Bright Medusa*

2. All members of the staff wore plastic tags bearing their names and color photographs.

Laurie Colwin, "Animal Behavior"

3. Jerry stood on the landing.

Joyce Carol Oates, *The Wheel of Love and Other Stories*

4. They lived in a square two-flat house tightly packed among identical houses in a fog-enveloped street in the Sunset district of San Francisco.

William Saroyan, "Boy and Girls Together"

Add Two Expansions

5. His teeth were pitifully inadequate by comparison with the mighty fighting fangs of the anthropoids.

Edgar Rice Burroughs, "Tarzan's First Love"

6. He used to ride, alone.

Nancy Hale, "The Rider Was Lost"

7. She tossed her book to the desk and hurried to the rail.

F. Scott Fitzgerald, *Flappers and Philosophers*

8. It is hardly surprising that so many people lose their tempers with so many other people.

Shirley Jackson, "About Two Nice People"

PRACTICE 5

Each sentence is a reduced version of a professionally written sentence. You're not told the number, position, and length of the expansions. You must decide all three. After you've finished, compare your sentences with those of the professional authors in the References on page 138. Note similarities and dissimilarities in the number, the position, and the length of the expansions.

The only guideline given is the number of words in the original sentence. Try to expand the reduced sentence to approximately the same length as the original.

1. He can feel the eyes on him. (14 words)

Judith Guest, Original People

2. She made the best meatloaf in the world. (24 words)

Nancy Friday, My Mother/My Self

3. Weary made Billy take a very close look at his trench knife. (27 words)

Kurt Vonnegut, Jr., Slaughter-House Five

4. The gardens were laid out so neatly. (28 words)

Judith Guest, Ordinary People

5. A pale silk scarf is tied around his neck. (29 words)

Philip Roth, The Professor of Desire

6. The four animals continued to lead their lives. (30 words)

Kenneth Grahame, The Wind in the Willows

7. He went into the kitchen. (31 words)

Kurt Vonnegut, Jr., Slaughter-House Five

PRACTICE 6

Select 20 sentences from writing you have done recently. Choose 10 of the sentences to expand. For each, add at least one expansion. Vary the lengths, structures, and positions of the expansions.

II

Using Professional
Sentence Structures

The immediate goal of this part of the textbook is to have you practice using three structures that professional writers use frequently but students rarely. The ultimate goal is for you to become so familiar with these structures that you'll use them with naturalness and confidence in the sentences you compose.

The three structures—absolutes, appositives, and participles—are easy to learn; to become skilled in using them, however, requires frequent practice. You'll practice these structures by using the four sentence composing techniques you've worked with in the preceding part of the textbook:

SENTENCE SCRAMBLING
SENTENCE IMITATING
SENTENCE COMBINING
SENTENCE EXPANDING

5

Sentence Composing
with Absolute Phrases

IDENTIFYING THE SKILL

Here's a list of sentences, all written by professional writers, but with some parts deleted.

1. She returned to her bench.
2. The boy watched.
3. About the bones, ants were ebbing away.
4. Six boys came over the hill half an hour early that afternoon, running hard.

Now compare the above sentences with the originals. Notice that the part deleted, when combined with the reduced sentence above, accounts for the distinctiveness of the original sentence.

1a. She returned to her bench, **her face showing all the unhappiness that had suddenly overtaken her.**

Theodore Dreiser, An American Tragedy

2a. The boy watched, **his eyes bulging in the dark**.

Edmund Ware, "An Underground Episode"

3a. About the bones, ants were ebbing away, **their pincers full of meat.**

Doris Lessing, African Stories

4a. Six boys came over the hill half an hour early that afternoon, running hard, **their heads down, their forearms working, their breath whistling.**

John Steinbeck, The Red Pony

The **boldface** phrases are absolute phrases, one of the sentence parts that differentiates professional writing from student writing. They're frequently used by professional writers but rarely by students. Absolute phrases are an efficient way to combine related ideas in one sentence.

40

CHARACTERISTICS OF ABSOLUTE PHRASES

Definition

An absolute phrase is a modifier that grammatically resembles a complete sentence. Included in every absolute phrase is a subject and a partial verb, which is why it resembles a complete sentence. However, since the verb is only partial and not complete, absolutes are considered phrases and not clauses. Missing in every absolute phrase is an auxiliary verb—always a form of the verb *to be* (*is, are, was,* or *were*). Here are examples of absolute phrases with auxiliary verbs inserted (in parentheses) that would change the phrase into a complete sentence. The absolute phrases are taken from the above four sentences.

1a. Her face (was) showing all the happiness that had suddenly overtaken her.

2a. His eyes (were) bulging in the dark.

3a. Their pincers (were) full of meat.

4a. Their heads (were) down. Their forearms (were) working. Their breath (was) whistling.

Another distinguishing characteristic of most absolute phrases is the kind of word they usually begin with. In all of the absolute phrases above, a possessive pronoun is the starting word:

1a. *her*

2a. *his*

3a. *their*

4a. *their*

The class of words called possessive pronouns has only a few members: *my, your, his, her, its, our,* and *their.* In absolute phrases the possessive pronoun is usually stated, but sometimes it's implied. In the first sentence below, the possessive pronoun that starts the absolute phrase is stated; in the second, it's implied.

Stated

Noiselessly Lenny appeared in the open doorway and stood there looking in, his big shoulders nearly filling the opening.

John Steinbeck, *Of Mice and Men*

Implied

The good dogs came stiffly out of their little house, [their] hackles up and deep growls in their throats.

John Steinbeck, *The Red Pony*

In summary, there are two ways to identify absolute phrases: (1) the phrase always can be changed into a sentence by adding an auxiliary verb—usually *was* or *were*—and (2) frequently, but not always, the starting word in the absolute phrase is a possessive pronoun, stated or implied.

Position

An absolute phrase can be used as a sentence opener (precedes a clause), S-V split (splits the subject and verb of a clause), or sentence closer (follows a clause).

Punctuation

When the absolute phrase is a sentence opener, a comma follows it.

His head aching, his throat sore, he forgot to light the cigarette.

Sinclair Lewis, Cass Timberlane

When the absolute phrase is an S-V split, commas precede and follow it.

Miss Hearne, **her face burning,** hardly listened to these words.

Brian Moore, The Lonely Passion of Judith Hearne

When the absolute phrase is a sentence closer, a comma precedes the phrase and a period follows it.

Light flickered on bits of ruby glass and on sensitive capillary hairs in the nylon-brushed nostrils of the creature that quivered gently, gently, **its eight legs spidered under it on rubber-padded paws.**

Ray Bradbury, Fahrenheit 451

PRACTICE 1

Each of the professionally written sentences below contains an absolute phrase. For each sentence, do the following:

a. Identify the absolute phrase and test your identification by changing the phrase into a complete sentence by adding the appropriate auxiliary verb (*was* or *were*).

b. Indicate the possessive pronoun that starts the absolute phrase. Where the possessive pronoun is implied rather than stated, identify the intended pronoun.

c. State the position of the absolute phrase (sentence opener, S-V split, sentence closer).

Answers are in the References on page 138.

1. High in the air, a little figure, his hands thrust in his short jacket pockets, stood staring out to sea.

Katherine Mansfield, "The Voyage"

2. He walked with a prim strut, swinging out his legs in a half-circle with each step, his heels biting smartly into the red velvet carpet on the floor.

Carson McCullers, "The Jockey"

3. Outside, his carpetbag in his hand, he stood for a time in the barnyard.

Jessamyn West, "A Time of Learning"

4. Father lay crumped up on the stone floor of the pantry, face down, arms twisted at a curious angle....

Christy Brown, *Down All the Days*

PRACTICING THE SKILL: SENTENCE SCRAMBLING

PRACTICE 2

Although most absolute phrases begin with possessive pronouns (*my, your, his, her, its, our, their*), some do not. Here are examples:

a. He hoisted the sack of feed and took it into the wire dogpen, the **bird dogs crowding around him,** rearing up on him in their eagerness.

Borden Deal, "The Christmas Hunt"

b. Generally, ships sailed in long convoys, **merchant ship after merchant ship,** like trains of vessels on the water strung out almost as far as the eye could see.

Edward Rome Snow, "The Light at South Point"

To identify absolute phrases, use the test that applies to every absolute phrase. If you can change it into a sentence by adding *was* or *were*, it's an absolute phrase.

a. The bird dogs [were] crowding around him.
b. Merchant ship [was] after merchant ship.

Each of the scrambled sentences below contains an absolute phrase that doesn't begin with a possessive pronoun. First, identify the sentence part that is the absolute phrase. Next, unscramble each sentence to produce the most effective arrangement of the sentence parts. Punctuate correctly. When you finish, compare your sentences with the originals in the References on page 139. Which do you like better? Why?

1a. was awake for quite a long time
b. the moonlight on her face
c. thinking about things
d. I
e. and watching Catherine sleeping

Ernest Hemingway, *A Farewell to Arms*

2a. each child carrying his little bag of crackling
 b. we
 c. in the cold winter afternoon
 d. trod the long road home
 e. one of many small groups of children

Peter Abrahams, Tell Freedom

3a. I
 b. each set upon a carved wooden base
 c. looked across to a lighted case of Chinese design
 d. which held delicate-looking statues
 e. of horses and birds, small vases and bowls

Ralph Ellison, Invisible Man

PRACTICE 3

Each of the scrambled sentences below contains more than one absolute phrase. Unscramble each sentence to produce the most effective arrangement of the sentence parts. Punctuate correctly. When you finish, compare your sentences with the originals in the References on page 139. Which do you like better? Why?

1a. while Buck struggled in fury
 b. then the rope tightened mercilessly
 c. and his great chest panting
 d. his tongue lolling out of his mouth

Jack London, The Call of the Wild

2a. wherever it settled its weight
 b. it ran
 c. its taloned feet clawing damp earth
 d. leaving prints six inches deep
 e. its pelvic bones crushing aside trees and bushes

Ray Bradbury, "A Sound of Thunder"

3a. her shoulders drooping a little
 b. her glasses winking in the sunlight
 c. she was now standing
 d. arms akimbo
 e. her head cocked to one side

Harper Lee, To Kill a Mockingbird

4a. as if he could squeal or laugh out loud
 b. and then
 c. his hand in one pocket clutching the money
 d. he felt
 e. his feet sinking in the soft nap of the carpet

Theodore Dreiser, An American Tragedy

5a. you could hear the signs and murmurs as the furthest chambers
   of it died
 b. closing up forever
 c. the organs malfunctioning
 d. everything shutting off
 e. liquids running a final instant from pocket to sac to spleen

Ray Bradbury, "A Sound of Thunder"

PRACTICING THE SKILL: SENTENCE IMITATING

PRACTICE 4

Underneath the model sentence are two imitations. Both the model
and the imitations contain absolute phrases. The imitations are presented as a list of scrambled sentence parts for you to unscramble to
duplicate the structure of the model. Unscramble each of the two
sentences to produce a sentence similar in structure to the model.
Identify the sentence part that is the absolute phrase in the scrambled list.
Compare your sentences with the ones in the References on page 139.

Model

The motorcycle on the sidewalk speeded up and skidded obliquely
into a plate-glass window, the front wheel bucking and climbing the
brick base beneath the window.

Frank Rooney, "Cyclist's Raid"

Scrambled Imitations

1a. the other customers rallying and demanding the same reduction in the cost
 b. one customer in the line spoke out
 c. about the unfair price
 d. and ranted continuously

2a. and moved quickly
 b. one couple heading and leading the rest through the complicated steps
 c. into two lines
 d. several dancers near the band joined together

PRACTICE 5

First, read the model several times, paying special attention to the
structure of the sentence. In each model the absolute phrase is in
boldface. Study it. Also, study the rest of the sentence carefully; you'll

need to be familiar with not only the absolute phrase but also the rest of the sentence structure.

Next, read the list of sentences underneath the model. Combine these into one sentence having basically the same structure as the model. The order in which the sentences are listed is the order of the parts of the model. In other words, convert the first sentence into the first sentence part of the model, the second sentence into the second part, and so forth. Compare yours with the ones in the References on page 140.

Finally, write an imitation of the model, keeping the same structure but providing your own content.

EXAMPLE

Model

He returned, shuddering, five minutes later, **his arms soaked and red to the elbows.**

Ray Bradbury, "A Sound of Thunder"

Sentences to Be Combined

a. This is about the soldiers.
b. They retreated.
c. They were shivering.
d. This happened two days ago.
e. Their spirits were outraged.
f. In addition, their spirits were crushed.
g. This effect on their spirits was caused by the defeat.

Combination

The soldiers retreated, shivering, two days ago, **their spirits outraged and crushed by the defeat.**

Imitation

She left, smiling, a minute before, **her Andrew Wyeth print matted and framed in green.**

---

1. *Model:* The electric train was there waiting, **all the lights on.**

Ernest Hemingway, A Farewell to Arms

a. The youngest brother was nearby.
b. He was resting.
c. All his work was over.

2. *Model:* As soon as she was well, we went to Southend-on-the-

Sea for a holiday, **Mother outfitting us completely with new clothes.**

Charles Spencer Chaplin (Charlie Chaplin), My *Autobiography*

a. It happened as soon as ıt was over.
b. What happened then was that they pranced around Gracie.
c. They did their prancing like courtiers.
d. Paul was wooing her disgustingly.
e. He wooed her with his stretched smiles.

3. *Model:* Then, very afraid, she shook her head warningly, and touched a finger to her lips and shook her head again, **her eyes pleading with him.**

James Clavell, *Shogun*

a. Later, he was somewhat sorry.
b. He held the baby.
c. He held it soothingly.
d. In addition, he brought the music box to her.
e. He wound the toy up.
f. His voice was singing with it.

4. *Model:* The old woman pointed upwards interrogatively and, on my aunt's nodding, proceeded to toil up the narrow staircase before us, **her bowed head being scarcely above the level of the banister-rail.**

James Joyce, "The Sisters"

a. The student teacher erased everything quickly.
b. In addition, she did something with a hurried cover-up.
c. She started to call out the spelling words.
d. She did this for us.
e. Her embarrassment was definitely coming from something.
f. It was coming from her misspelling.
g. The misspelling was on the chalkboard.

PRACTICE 6

The model sentences are arranged in groups according to the position of the absolute phrase. Using the structure of the model sentence but your own content, write a sentence imitation for each of the models below. Imitate the structure of the entire sentence, not just the absolute phrase.

Sentence Openers

1. Outside, **his carpet bag in his hand,** he stood for a time in the barnyard.

Jessamyn West, "A Time of Learning"

2. His head aching, his throat sore, he forgot to light the cigarette.

Sinclair Lewis, Cass Timberlane

3. A moment later, his hands upraised, his pony's bridle reins caught in the crook of one arm, a young man moved into the zone of light that shone bravely out through Tim Geogehan's back window.

F. R. Buckley, "Gold-Mounted Guns"

S-V Splits

4. A seared man, his charred clothes fuming where the blast had blown out the fire, rose from the curb.

Fritz Leiber, "A Bad Day for Sales "

5. Some got out, their bodies burnt and flattened, and went off not knowing where they were going.

Ernest Hemingway, A Farewell to Arms

6. Mammoth Mister Victor Mature, sweat streaming down his face, met and held the lion, bigger now as the close-up showed its mammoth jaws, its mammoth fangs.

Brian Moore, The Lonely Passion of Judith Hearne

Sentence Closers

7. A water snake slipped along on the pool, its head held up like a little periscope.

John Steinbeck, Of Mice and Men

8. Jack stood up as he said this, the bloodied knife in his hands.

William Golding, Lord of the Flies

9. My brother came to my side, his eyes drawn by the blazing straws.

Richard Wright, Native Son

PRACTICING THE SKILL: SENTENCE COMBINING

PRACTICE 7

In the first sentence in each group, a slash mark (/) indicates that the original sentence has an absolute phrase at that place. Combine the rest of the sentences into an absolute phrase that will fit smoothly into the place indicated by the slash mark. Compare your results with the originals in the References on page 140. Write an imitation of the resulting sentences, using your own content and the structure of the model.

EXAMPLE

a. She slid back the roof of the cockpit once again, / .
b. Her nose was wrinkling.
c. It was wrinkling at the rankness of the morass.
d. The morass was dripping.
e. The morass was encircling them.

Combination with Absolute Phrase

She slid back the roof of the cockpit once again, **her nose wrinkling at the rankness of the dripping morass encircling them.**

Alan Dean Foster, "Splinter of the Mind's Eye"

Imitation

He climbed down the limb of the cherry tree very slowly, **his arms tightening around the bark of the big branch supporting him.**

1a. The town lay on a broad estuary, / .
  b. The town's old yellow plastered buildings were hugging something.
  c. The buildings were hugging the beach.

Based on a sentence by John Steinbeck, The Pearl

2a. Like giants they toiled, / .
  b. The days were flashing on the heels of days like dreams.
  c. This happened as they heaped the treasure up.

Based on a sentence by Jack London, The Call of the Wild

3a. An Arab on a motorcycle, / , passed John at such a clip that the spirals of dust from his turnings on the winding road looked like little tornadoes.
  b. The Arab's robes were flying.
  c. The robes were long.
  d. The robes were flying in the wind.
  e. The wind was of his speed.

Based on a sentence by Elizabeth Yates, "Standing in Another's Shoes"

4a. In solid phalanxes the leaders crowded about the three jaguars, / , / . (two absolute phrases)
  b. Their tusks were thrust.
  c. The thrusting was forward.
  d. Their little eyes were bloodshot with anger.
  e. In addition, they were bloodshot with battle lust.

Based on a sentence by Jack London, The Call of the Wild

PRACTICE 8

Combine each list of sentences into one sentence containing an absolute phrase. Underline each phrase. You may eliminate words and change their form as long as the intended meaning remains. Punctuate correctly. When you finish, compare your sentences with the originals in the References on page 140.

1a. I could hear him.
  b. He was crashing down the hill.
  c. He was crashing toward the sea.
  d. The frightening laughter was echoing back.

Based on a sentence by Theodore Taylor, The Cay

2a. Finny and I went along the Boardwalk.
  b. We were in our sneakers and white slacks.
  c. Finny was in a light blue polo shirt.
  d. I was in a T-shirt.

Based on a sentence by John Knowles, A Separate Peace

3a. It happened all the time he was reading the newspaper.
  b. What happened was that his wife leaned out of the window.
  c. His wife was a fat woman with a white face.
  d. She was gazing into the street.
  e. Her thick white arms were folded under her loose breast on the window sill.

Based on a sentence by Bernard Malamud, "A Summer's Reading"

4a. To the right of them the gym meditated.
  b. It meditated behind its gray walls.
  c. The windows were shining back at the sun.
  d. The windows were high.
  e. The windows were wide.
  f. The windows were oval-topped.

Based on a sentence by John Knowles, A Separate Peace

PRACTICING THE SKILL: SENTENCE EXPANDING

PRACTICE 9

Expand the sentences by adding aproximately the same number of words the authors used for their absolute phrases. The number is next to the slash mark (/). To help you start, the beginning words of the absolute phrases are provided in **boldface**. Compare your absolute phrases with the originals in the References on page 141.

1. Now, in the waning daylight, he turned into Glover Street toward his home, /10 **his arms**. . . .

Norman Katkov, "The Torn Invitation"

2. As they drove off, Wilson saw her standing under the big tree, looking pretty rather than beautiful in her faintly rosy khaki, /17 **her dark hair**. . . , /12 **her face**. . . .

Ernest Hemingway, "The Short Happy Life of Francis Macomber"

3. His great chest was low to the ground, /5 **his head**. . . , /5 **his feet**. . . , /10 **the claws**. . . .

Jack London, *The Call of the Wild*

4. In front of the house where we lived, the mountain went down steeply to the little plain along the lake, and we sat on the porch of the house in the sun and saw the winding of the road down the mountain-side and the terraced vineyards on the side of the lower mountain, /8 **the vines** . . . and /6 **the fields** . . . , and below the vineyards, /13 **the houses**. . . .

Ernest Hemingway, *A Farewell to Arms*

PRACTICE 10

Add an absolute phrase to each of the reduced sentences below, blending your content with the rest of the sentence. Each of the sentences in its original, complete version had an absolute phrase in the place indicated by the slash mark (/). When you finish, compare your sentences with the originals in the References on page 141.

Practice a variety of lengths for your absolute phrases. Don't be disappointed if your content is unlike that of the original. Try to imagine content that will work well when blended with the rest of the author's sentence.

1. He began scrambling up the wooden pegs nailed to the side of the tree, / .

John Knowles, *A Separate Peace*

2. Touser roused himself under Fowler's desk and scratched another flea, / .

Clifford D. Simak, "Desertion"

3. They were smiling, / , / .

Jack Finney, "Of Missing Persons"

4. Men, / , / , swung by; a few women all muffled scurried along; and one tiny boy, / , was jerked along angrily between his father and mother; he looked like a baby fly that had fallen into the cream.

Katherine Mansfield, "The Voyage"

PRACTICE 11

Revise a piece of your recent writing by expanding selected sentences using absolute phrases. Vary the position, length, and number of absolute phrases.

6

Sentence Composing
with Appositive Phrases

IDENTIFYING THE SKILL

Here's a list of sentences, all written by professional writers, but with some parts deleted.

1. It went away slowly.
2. The land that lay stretched out before him became a vast significance.
3. However, I looked with a mixture of admiration and awe at Peter.
4. That night in the south upstairs chamber Emmett lay in a kind of trance.

Now compare the above sentences with the originals. Notice that the parts deleted, when combined with the reduced sentences above, account for the distinctiveness of the original sentences.

1a. It went away slowly, **the feeling of disappointment that came sharply after the thrill that made his shoulders ache.**

Ernest Hemingway, "Big Two-Hearted River: Part II"

2a. The land that lay stretched out before him became of vast significance, **a place peopled by his fancy with a new race of men sprung from himself.**

Sherwood Anderson, Winesburg, Ohio

3a. However, I looked with a mixture of admiration and awe at Peter, **a boy who could and did imitate a police siren every morning on his way to the showers.**

Robert Russell, To Catch an Angel

4a. That night in the south upstairs chamber, **a hot little room where a full-leafed chinaberry tree shut all the air from the single window,** Emmett lay in a kind of trance.

Jessamyn West, "A Time of Learning"

The **boldface** phrases are appositives, another of the sentence parts that differentiate professional writing from student writing. They're frequently used by professional writers but rarely by students. Appositive phrases are an efficient way to combine related ideas in one sentence.

CHARACTERISTICS OF APPOSITIVE PHRASES

Definition

An appositive is a noun or (much less often) pronoun that identifies an adjacent noun or pronoun. An appositive phrase is the appositive word plus any of its modifiers. Here are examples. The complete appositive phrase is in **boldface**.

1. Poppa, **a good quiet man,** spent the last hours before our parting moving aimlessly about the yard, keeping to himself and avoiding me.

   Gordon Parks, "My Mother's Dream for Me"

2. The boy looked at them, **big black ugly insects.**

   Doris Lessing, *African Stories*

3. Hour after hour he stood there, silent, motionless, **a shadow carved in ebony and moonlight.**

   James V. Marshall, *Walkabout*

4. A man, **a weary old pensioner with a bald dirty head and a stained brown corduroy waistcoat,** appeared at the door of a small gate lodge.

   Brian Moore, *The Lonely Passion of Judith Hearne*

5. He had the appearance of a man who had done a great thing, **something greater than any ordinary man would do.**

   John Henrik Clarke, "The Boy Who Painted Christ Black"

Position

An appositive phrase can be used as a sentence opener (precedes a clause), S-V split (splits the subject and verb of a clause), or sentence closer (follows a clause).

Punctuation

When the appositive phrase is a sentence opener, a comma follows it.

One of eleven brothers and sisters, Harriet was a moody, willful child.

Langston Hughes, "Road to Freedom"

When the appositive phrase is an S-V split, commas precede and follow it.

Van'ka Zhukov, **a boy of nine who had been apprenticed to the shoemaker Alyakhin three months ago,** was staying up that Christmas Eve.

Anton Chekhov, "Van'ka"

When the appositive phrase is a sentence closer, a comma precedes the phrase and a period follows it.

At once Fujiko got up and motioned him to wait as she rushed noiselessly for the swords that lay in front of the takonama, **the little alcove of honor.**

James Clavell, Shogun

PRACTICE 1

Each of the professionally written sentences below contains an appositive phrase. For each sentence, do the following:

a. Identify the appositive phrase.
b. Name the word the appositive phrase identifies.
c. State the position of the appositive phrase (sentence opener, S-V split, sentence closer).

Answers are in the References on page 141.

1. The writer, an old man with a white mustache, had some difficulty in getting into bed.

Sherwood Anderson, Winesburg, Ohio

2. Halfway there he heard the sound he dreaded, the hollow, rasping cough of a horse.

John Steinbeck, The Red Pony

3. Mr. Mick Malloy, cashier at the Ulster and Connaught Bank, draped his grey sports jacket neatly on a hanger and put on his black shantung work coat.

Brian Moore, The Lonely Passion of Judith Hearne

4. A self-educated man, he had accepted the necessary smattering facts of science with a serene indulgence, as simply so much further proof of what the Creator could do when He put His hand to it.

Wilbur Daniel Steele, "The Man Who Saw Through Heaven"

PRACTICING THE SKILL: SENTENCE SCRAMBLING

PRACTICE 2

Each of the scrambled sentences below contains an appositive phrase. First, identify the sentence part that is the appositive phrase. Next, unscramble each sentence to produce the most effective arrangement of the sentence parts. Punctuate correctly. When you finish, compare your sentences with the originals in the References on page 142. Which do you like better? Why?

1a. struggled as usual
  b. she
  c. to maintain her calm, composed, friendly bearing
  d. a sort of mask she wore all over her body

D. H. Lawrence, "The Blind Man"

2a. an old, bowlegged fellow in a pale-blue sweater
  b. the judge
  c. and was reading over some notes he had taken
  d. had stopped examining the animals
  e. on the back of a dirty envelope

Jessamyn West, "The Lesson"

3a. of a small gate lodge
  b. appeared
  c. a weary old pensioner with a bald dirty head and a stained brown corduroy waistcoat
  d. a man
  e. at the door

Brian Moore, The Lonely Passion of Judith Hearne

PRACTICE 3

Each of the scrambled sentences below contains more than one appositive phrase. Unscramble each sentence to produce the most effective arrangement of the sentence parts. Punctuate correctly. When you finish, compare your sentences with the originals in the References on page 142. Which do you like better? Why?

1a. talked continually of virginity
  b. the son of a jeweler in Winesburg
  c. one of them
  d. a slender young man with white hands

Sherwood Anderson, Winesburg, Ohio

2a. went over to Tom Willy's saloon

b. in the late afternoon
c. Will Henderson
d. and editor of the *Eagle*
e. owner

Sherwood Anderson, Winesburg, Ohio

3a. and the jingle of trace chains
b. was louder
c. drag of brakes
d. the sound of the approaching grain teams
e. thud of big hooves on hard ground.

John Steinbeck, Of Mice and Men

4a. with the butt of a teamster's whip
b. once Enoch Bentley
c. old Tom Bentley
d. struck his father
e. and the old man seemed likely to die
f. the older one of the boys

Sherwood Anderson, Winesburg, Ohio

5a. with devil-may-care eyes and a long humorous nose
b. Mr. Mick Malloy
c. tall cashier with a dignified face
d. a nice sort of fellow
e. tall, young secret gambler
f. a gentlemanly bank clerk
g. became Mr. Malloy

Brian Moore, The Lonely Passion of Judith Hearne

PRACTICING THE SKILL: SENTENCE IMITATING

PRACTICE 4

Underneath the model sentence are two imitations. Both the model and the imitations contain appositive phrases. The imitations are presented as a list of scrambled sentence parts for you to unscramble to duplicate the structure of the model. Unscramble each of the two sentences to produce a sentence similar in structure to the model. Identify the sentence part that is the appositive phrase in the scrambled list. Compare your sentences with the ones in the References on page 142.

Model

Beside the fireplace old Doctor Winter sat, bearded and simple and benign, **historian and physician to the town.**

John Steinbeck, The Moon Is Down

Scrambled Imitations

1a. president and valedictorian of the senior class
 b. by the podium
 c. intelligent and composed and smiling
 d. scholarly Henrietta stood

2a. beaming and affectionate and happy
 b. bride and groom in their finery
 c. they danced
 d. under the canopy

PRACTICE 5

First, read the model several times, paying special attention to the structure of the sentence. In each model the appositive phrase is in **boldface**. Study it. Also, study the rest of the sentence carefully; you'll need to be familiar with not only the appositive phrase but also the rest of the sentence structure.

Next, read the list of sentences underneath the model. Combine these into one sentence having basically the same structure as the model. The order in which the sentences are listed is the order of the parts of the model. In other words, convert the first sentence into the first sentence part of the model, the second sentence into the second part, and so forth. Compare yours with the ones in the References on page 143.

Finally, write an imitation of the model, keeping the same structure but providing your own content.

EXAMPLE

Model

Mr. Cattanzara, **a stocky, bald-headed man who worked in a change booth on an IRT station,** lived on the next block after George's, above a shoe repair store.

Bernard Malamud, "A Summer's Reading"

Sentences to Be Combined

a. This is about Jan Carter.
b. She is an unabashed, sun-tanned flirt.
c. She had smiled at him in the cafeteria line.
d. She transferred to the department near Tom's.
e. She transferred for a "chance" meeting.

Combination

Jan Carter, **an unabashed, sun-tanned flirt who had smiled at him in the cafeteria line,** transferred to the department near Tom's, for a "chance" meeting.

Imitation

Tom Zengler, **the slower, more heavy-handed pianist who had studied under Professor Samione for a decade,** performed in the recital hall near Jacob's, with an obvious competitive attitude.

---

1. *Model:* Among the company was a lawyer, **a young man of about twenty-five.**

Anton Chekhov, "The Bet"

a. She was near the statue.
b. She was an obvious tourist.
c. She was an oriental lady.
d. She had a Kodak camera.

2. *Model:* Sady Ellison, **the daughter of Long Butt Ellison,** worked as a waitress for Turkey Plott in a defiant and condescending fashion.

Wayne Kernodle, "Last of the Rugged Individualists"

a. This is about *Gone with the Wind.*
b. That is the movie with the most re-issues.
c. It originated as a novel.
d. The novel was of the old South.
e. The novel was by someone who was un-glamorous.
f. The someone was also unknown.
g. The someone was an authoress.

3. *Model:* Captain Bentick was a family man, **a lover of dogs and pink children and Christmas.**

John Steinbeck, *The Moon Is Down*

a. "Missouri" is a casserole.
b. The casserole is special.
c. It is a blend of several ingredients.
d. It has potatoes.
e. It has tomatoes.
f. The tomatoes are stewed.
g. It has hamburger.

4. *Model:* He was close to twenty and had needs with the neighborhood girls, but no money to spend, and he couldn't get more than an occasional few cents because his father was poor, and his sister Sophie, who resembled George, **a tall, bony girl of twenty-three,** earned very little, and what she had she kept for herself.

Bernard Malamud, "A Summer's Reading"

a. We were far from our destination.
b. In addition, we were making good time on the interstate.
c. But there was no time to squander.
d. In addition, Dad wouldn't stop more than twice a day.
e. Although we kids were itchy, he wouldn't stop.
f. In addition, Mom was the one who kept the peace.
g. She was a shrewd, gentle arbitrator.
h. She had Solomon's mind.
i. She circumvented some flare-ups.
j. And she did something with those she couldn't circumvent.
k. She left those to Heaven.

PRACTICE 6

The model sentences are arranged in groups according to the position of the appositive phrase. Using the structure of the model sentence but your own content, write a sentence imitation for each of the models below. Imitate the structure of the entire sentence, not just the appositive phrase.

Sentence Openers

1. **One of eleven brothers and sisters,** Harriet was a moody, willful child.

Langston Hughes, "Road to Freedom"

2. **A self-educated man,** he had accepted the necessary smattering facts of science with a serene indulgence, as simply so much further proof of what the Creator could do when He put His Hand to it.

Wilbur Daniel Steele, "The Man Who Saw Through Heaven"

S-V Splits

3. One of these, **a young woman who turned to look,** called to Yakov, but by then the wagon was out of the marketplace, scattering some chickens nesting in the ruts of the road and a flock of jabbering ducks, as it clattered on.

Bernard Malamud, *The Fixer*

4. Henry Strader, **an old man who had been on the farm since Jesse came into possession and who before David's time had never been known to make a joke,** made the same joke every morning.

Sherwood Anderson, Winesburg, Ohio

Sentence Closers

5. In all the years which have since elapsed, she remains the woman I loved and lost, **the unattainable one.**

Henry Miller, Stand Still Like a Hummingbird

6. It had a black spot on it, **the black spot Mr. Summer had made the night before with the heavy pencil in the coal-company office.**

Shirley Jackson, "The Lottery"

PRACTICING THE SKILL: SENTENCE COMBINING

PRACTICE 7

In the first sentence in each group, a slash mark (/) indicates that the original sentence had an appositive phrase at that place. Combine the sentences underneath into an appositive phrase that will fit smoothly into the place indicated by the slash mark. Compare your results with the originals in the References on page 143. Write an imitation of the resulting sentence, using your own content and the structure of the model.

EXAMPLE

a. She was playing the Canteen at Aldershot at the time, / .
b. The theatre was grubby.
c. The theatre was mean.
d. The theatre was catering mostly to soldiers.

Combination with Appositive Phrase

She was playing the Canteen at the Aldershot at the time, **a grubby, mean theatre catering mostly to soldiers.**

Charles Spencer Chaplin (Charlie Chaplin), My Autobiography

Imitation

He was inspecting a condemned school near Thorn Road around noon, **an old, stone building closing probably in June.**

1a. On this Sunday morning the postman and the policeman had gone fishing in the boat of Mr. Corell, / .
  b. Mr. Corell was the store-keeper.
  c. He was popular.

Based on a sentence by John Steinbeck, The Moon Is Down

2a. The real estate agent, / , soon joined them.
  b. The agent was a man.
  c. He was old.
  d. He had a face.
  e. The face was smiling.
  f. The face was hypocritical.

Based on a sentence by Willa Cather, "The Sculptor's Funeral"

3a. They approached the domed synagogue with its iron weathercock, / , for the time being resting in peace.
  b. The synagogue was a yellow-walled building.
  c. It was pock-marked.
  d. It had a door.
  e. The door was oak.

Based on a sentence by Bernard Malamud, The Fixer

4a. Lieutenant Tonder was a poet, / .
  b. He was a bitter poet.
  c. He was a poet who dreamed of perfect, ideal love.
  d. The love was of elevated young men for girls.
  e. The girls were poor.

Based on a sentence by John Steinbeck, The Moon Is Down

PRACTICE 8

Combine each list of sentences into one sentence containing an appositive phrase. Underline each phrase. You may eliminate words and change their form as long as the intended meaning remains. Punctuate correctly. When you finish, compare your sentences with the originals in the References on page 143.

1a. Something happens at the gate.
  b. There, I show the pass to a private.
  c. The private is young.
  d. The private is Japanese.
  e. The private is the sentry.

Based on a sentence by Richard E. Kim, Lost Names

2a. It happened when he was twelve.
  b. Then, his mother married an executive.
  c. The executive was of a machine tool company.
  d. The company was in Cleveland.

e. The executive was an engineer.
f. He was an engineer who had adult children of his own.

Based on a sentence by Glendon Swarthout, *Bless the Beasts and Children*

3a. My patient was a woman.
b. She was modern.
c. She was intelligent.
d. She with her five children seemed trapped.
e. She seemed as trapped as her forebears.
f. Her forebears were in Victorian times.
g. In Victorian times was before the emanicipation of women.

Based on a sentence by Rollo May, *Love and Will*

4a. On the bark of the tree was scored something.
b. What was scored there was a name.
c. The name was of Deacon Peabody.
d. Deacon Peabody was a man.
e. He was eminent.
f. It was he who had waxed wealthy.
g. He did this by driving bargains.
h. The bargains were shrewd.
i. The bargains were with the Indians.

Based on a sentence by Washington Irving, "The Devil and Tom Walker"

PRACTICING THE SKILL: SENTENCE EXPANDING

PRACTICE 9

Expand the sentences by adding approximately the same number of words the authors used for their appositive phrases. The number is next to the slash mark (/). To help you start, the beginning words of the appositive phrases are provided in **boldface**. Compare your appositive phrases with the originals in the References on page 143.

1. Thus, one noontime, coming back from the office lunch downstairs a little earlier than usual, he found her and several of the foreign-family girls, as well as four of the American girls, surrounding Polish Mary, / 11 **one of the** ..., who was explaining in rather a high key how a certain "feller" whom she had met the night before had given her a beaded bag, and for what purpose.

Theodore Dreiser, *An American Tragedy*

2. The rest were standing around in hatless, smoky little groups of twos and threes and fours inside the heated waiting room, talking in voices that, almost without exception, sounded col-

legiately dogmatic, as though each young man, in his strident, conversational turn, was clearing up, once and for all, some highly controversial issue, /14 **one that.** . . .

J. D. Salinger, Franny and Zooey

3. Out in the distances the fans of windmills twinkled, turning, and about the base of each, about the drink tank, was a speckle of dark dots, /17 **a gather of cattle.** . . .

Glendon Swarthout, Bless the Beasts and Children

4. Perhaps two or three times a year we would come together at a party, one of those teen-age affairs which last until dawn with singing and dancing and silly game such as "Kiss the Pillow," or "Post Office," /21 **the game which.** . . .

Henry Miller, Stand Still Like a Hummingbird

PRACTICE 10

Add an appositive phrase to each of the reduced sentences below, blending your content with the rest of the sentence. Each of the sentences in its original, complete version had an appositive phrase in the place indicated by the slash mark. When you finish, compare your sentences with the originals in the References on page 144.

Practice a variety of lengths for your appositive phrases. Don't be disappointed if your content is unlike that of the original. Try to imagine content that will work well when blended with the rest of the author's sentence.

1. My bed was an army cot, / .

James Thurber, "The Night the Bed Fell"

2. He, / , had fled because of superior perceptions and knowledge.

Stephen Crane, The Red Badge of Courage

3. I had hardly any patience with the serious work of life which, not that it stood between me and desire, seemed to me child's play, / .

James Joyce, "Araby"

4. There was Major Hunter, / , / . (two appositive phrases)

John Steinbeck, The Moon Is Down

PRACTICE 11

Revise a piece of your recent writing by expanding selected sentences using appositive phrases. Vary the position, length, and number of the phrases.

7

Sentence Composing
with Participle Phrases

IDENTIFYING THE SKILL

Here's a list of sentences, all written by professional writers, but with some parts deleted.

1. We could see the lake and the mountains across the lake on the French side.
2. Sadao had his reward.
3. The sun rose clear and bright.
4. Spencer took half an hour.

Now compare the above sentences with the originals. Notice that the part deleted, when combined with the reduced sentence above, accounts for the distinctiveness of the original sentence.

1a. Sitting up in bed eating breakfast, we could see the lake and the mountains across the lake on the French side.

Ernest Hemingway, A Farewell to Arms

2a. Sadao, **searching the spot of black in the twilight sea that night,** had his reward.

Pearl S. Buck, "The Enemy"

3a. The sun rose clear and bright, **tinging the foamy crests of the waves with a reddish purple.**

Alexander Dumas, Count of Monte Cristo

4a. Spencer took half an hour, **swimming in one of the pools which was filled with the seasonal rain, waiting for the pursuers to catch up to him.**

Ray Bradbury, The Martian Chronicles

The **boldface** phrases are participles, one of the sentence parts that appears frequently in professional writing, but rarely in student writing. Participle phrases are an efficient way to combine related ideas into one sentence.

65

In the last two sections of this book, you studied two other structures (absolute phrases and appositive phrases) that are used frequently by professionals but infrequently by students. Even though those two structures are quite common in professional writing, this one (participle phrases) is the most common, occurring so frequently that you can find examples on almost any page of a book.

CHARACTERISTICS OF PARTICIPLE PHRASES

Definition

A participle phrase is a modifier of a noun or pronoun. The first word in the phrase is almost always the participle itself. There are two types of participles. Those called present participles always end in *ing*. Those called past participles almost always end in either *ed* or *en*. Below are examples of both, with the complete participle phrases in **boldface**, and the noun (or pronoun) modified by the phrase underlined. The participle is in SMALL CAPS.

Present Participles

1. She was quite far from the windows which were to her left, and behind her were a couple of tall bookcases, CONTAINING **all the books of the factory library.**

   John Hersey, *Hiroshima*

2. Minute fungi overspread the whole exterior, HANGING **in a fine tangled web-work from the eaves.**

   Edgar Allan Poe, "The Fall of the House of Usher"

3. STANDING **there in the middle of the street,** Marty suddenly thought of Halloween, of the winter and snowballs, of the schoolyard.

   Murray Heyert, "The New Kid"

4. Professor Kazan, WEARING **a spotlessly white tropical suit and a wide-brimmed hat,** was the first ashore.

   Arthur C. Clarke, *Dolphin Island*

5. He walked to the corner of the lot, then back again, STUDYING **the simple terrain as if deciding how best to effect an entry,** FROWNING **and** SCRATCHING **his head.**

   Harper Lee, *To Kill a Mockingbird*

Past Participles

6. In six months a dozen small towns had been laid down upon the

naked planet, FILLED **with sizzling neon tubes and yellow
electric bulbs.**

Ray Bradbury, The Martian Chronicles

7. The <u>tent,</u> ILLUMINED **by candle,** glowed warmly in the midst
of the plain.

Jack London, The Call of the Wild

8. ENCHANTED **and** ENTHRALLED, <u>I</u> stopped her constantly for
details.

Richard Wright, Black Boy

9. The other shoji slammed open, and UNSEEN, <u>Buntaro</u> stamped
away FOLLOWED **by the guard.**

James Clavell, Shogun

10. Her <u>hair,</u> BRAIDED **and** WRAPPED **around her head,** made
an ash-blonde crown.

John Steinbeck, The Grapes of Wrath

Position

A participle phrase can be used as a sentence opener (precedes a
clause), S-V split (splits the subject and verb of a clause), or sentence
closer (follows a clause)..

Sentence Openers

1. **Whistling,** he let the escalator waft him into the still night air.

Ray Bradbury, Fahrenheit 451

2. **Looking over their own troops,** they saw mixed masses
slowly getting into regular form.

Stephen Crane, The Red Badge of Courage

3. **Amazed at the simplicity of it all,** I understood everything as
never before.

Alphonse Daudet, "The Last Lesson"

S-V Splits

4. My father, **cautioning me not to work a horse till he had
fed fully,** said I had plenty of time to eat myself.

Lincoln Steffens, "A Boy on Horseback"

5. Eckels, **balanced on the narrow path,** aimed his rifle play-
fully.

Ray Bradbury, "A Sound of Thunder"

6. The sight of Mick's exploring beam of light, **flashing and
flickering through the submarine darkness a few yards
away,** reminded him that he was not alone.

Arthur C. Clarke, Dolphin Island

Sentence Closers

7. The entire crowd in the saloon gathered about me now, **urging me to drink.**

Richard Wright, Black Boy

8. She called to him, **excited.**

Daphne du Maurier, "The Birds"

9. The magician patted the hand, **holding it quietly with a thumb on its blue veins, waiting for life to revive.**

T. S. White, Book of Merlyn

Punctuation

When the participle phrase is a sentence opener, a comma follows it. When the participle phrase is an S-V split, commas precede and follow the phrase. When the participle phrase is a sentence closer, a comma precedes the phrase and a period follows it. (See the sentences above.)

PRACTICE 1

Each of the professionally written sentences below contains a participle phrase. For each sentence, do the following:

a. Identify the participle phrase and indicate the type of participle (present or past).
b. Name the word that the participle phrase modifies (describes).
c. State the position of the phrase (sentence opener, S-V split, or sentence closer).

Answers are in the References on page 145.

1. Manuel, lying on the ground, kicked at the bull's muzzle with his slippered feet.

Ernest Hemingway, "The Undefeated"

2. Clutching the clawing kitten to her collarbone, her hair in her open mouth, she bawled encouragement to them.

Elizabeth Enright, "Nancy"

3. They were diggers in clay, transformed by lantern light into a race of giants.

Edmund Ware, "An Underground Episode"

4. Ruthie, dressed in a real dress of pink muslin that came below her knees, was a little serious in her young-ladyness.

John Steinbeck, The Grapes of Wrath

PRACTICING THE SKILL: SENTENCE SCRAMBLING
PRACTICE 2

Sometimes the positions of participle phrases within a sentence are interchangeable: the same phrase could occur acceptably in any position—sentence opener, S-V split, or sentence closer. Which of the three to use will depend on such things as sentence variety, the relative emphasis desired, and the relation of the structure and content of the sentence to the other sentences in the paragraph. Sometimes, however, only two of the three positions (or only one of the three) are acceptable; the other positions would result in unacceptable grammar, poor modification, or lack of emphasis. The following Practice requires you to make the right decision about the positioning of participle phrases.

Unscramble each list of sentence parts three times: first, to produce a sentence with a participle phrase in the sentence opener position; next, in the S-V split position; and finally, in the sentence closer position. Classify the use of each position as either acceptable or unacceptable. If two positions are acceptable, or if all three are acceptable, discuss which position you prefer. Punctuate correctly. When you finish, compare your sentences with the originals in the References on page 145.

1a. was waiting on the landing outside
  b. Bernard
  c. wearing a black turtleneck sweater, dirty flannels, and slippers.

Brian Moore, *The Lonely Passion of Judith Hearne*

2a. could see the lake
  b. sitting up in bed eating breakfast
  c. we
  d. and the mountains across the lake on the French side

Ernest Hemingway, *A Farewell to Arms*

3a. coming down the pole
  b. with no control over my movements
  c. had a sense
  d. I
  e. of being whirled violently through the air.

Richard E. Byrd, *Alone*

4a. black
  b. a little house
  c. perched on high piles
  d. in the distance
  e. appeared

Joseph Conrad, "The Lagoon"

5a. screaming and begging to be allowed to go with her mother

   b. when we had made our way downstairs
   c. saw the woman with the lovely complexion
   d. Miss Pilzer
   e. we

Gerda Weissmann Klein, All But My Life

PRACTICE 3

Each of the scrambled sentences below contains more than one participle phrase. Unscramble each to produce the most effective arrangement of the sentence parts. Punctuate correctly. When you finish, compare your sentences with the originals in the References on page 147. Which do you like better? Why?

   1a. with the cautious, half-furtive effort of the sightless
   b. and thumping his way before him
   c. he was a blind beggar
   d. carrying the traditional battered cane

MacKinlay Kantor, "A Man Who Had No Eyes"

   2a. all had the look of invalids crawling into the hospital on their last legs
   b. the passengers
   c. blinking their eyes against the blinding sunlight
   d. emerging from the mildewed dimness of the customs sheds

Katherine Anne Porter, Ship of Fools

   3a. and yet knowing no way to avoid it
   b. that winter my mother and brother came
   c. buying furniture on the installment plan
   d. and we set up housekeeping
   e. being cheated

Richard Wright, Black Boy

   4a. where George Willard sat listening
   b. and breaking off the tale
   c. Doctor Parcival
   d. in the office of the Winesburg Eagle
   e. jumping to his feet
   f. began to walk up and down

Sherwood Anderson, Winesburg, Ohio

   5a. came up slowly
   b. his long embroidered robe streaming over her arm almost to the ground
   c. a young Mexican woman
   d. dressed in the elegant, perpetual mourning of her caste

e. who carried her baby
f. softened and dispirited by recent childbirth
g. leaning on the arm of the Indian nurse

Katherine Anne Porter, Ship of Fools

PRACTICING THE SKILL: SENTENCE IMITATING

PRACTICE 4

Underneath the model sentence are two imitations. Both the model and the imitations contain participles. The imitations are presented as a list of scrambled sentence parts for you to unscramble to duplicate the structure of the model. Unscramble each of the two sentences to produce a sentence similar in structure to the model. Identify the sentence parts that are participle phrases in the scrambled list. Compare your sentences with the ones in the References on page 147.

Model

As he ran away into the darkness, they repented of their weakness and ran after him, swearing and throwing sticks and great balls of soft mud at the figure that screamed and ran faster and faster into the darkness.

Sherwood Anderson, Winesburg, Ohio

Scrambled Imitations

1a. as her arm whirled fast over the egg-whites
b. and stared at it
c. and expressing confusion and frustration over the third direction in the recipe
d. her face shifted toward the cookbook
e. grimacing
f. that listed and explained more and ever more of the procedure

2a. stretching
b. that beckoned but hid farther and farther from his reach
c. after Jo-Jo climbed higher onto the counter
d. but missing jars and boxes in the rear with bright colors
e. he pulled on the doors
f. and looked for the candy

PRACTICE 5

First, read the model several times, paying special attention to the structure of the sentence. In each model the participle phrase is in boldface. Study it and the rest of the sentence carefully; you'll need to be familiar with not only the participle phrase but also the rest of the sentence structure.

Next, read the list of sentences underneath the model. Combine these into one sentence having basically the same structure as the model. The order in which the sentences are listed is the order of the parts of the model. In other words, convert the first sentence into the first sentence part of the model, the second sentence part into the second part, and so forth. Compare yours with the ones in the References on page 147.

Finally, write an imitation of the model, keeping the same structure but providing your own content.

EXAMPLE

Model

The horse found the entrance to the trail where it left the flat and started up, **stumbling and slipping on the rocks.**

John Steinbeck, "Flight"

Sentences to Be Combined

1. The cycle hit something.
2. It hit a stretch.
3. The stretch was ice.
4. It happened as it rounded the bend.
5. In addition, it slid sideways.
6. Then it was tottering.
7. In addition, then it was veering.
8. It was veering toward the shoulder.

Combination

The cycle hit a stretch of ice as it rounded the bend and slid sideways, **tottering and veering toward the shoulder.**

Imitation

His arm contacted the concrete of the schoolyard after he missed the jump and landed hard, **snapping and breaking at the impact.**

---

1. Model: The sound of monotonous ax blows rang through the forest, and the insects, **nodding upon their perches,** crooned like old women.

Stephen Crane, The Red Badge of Courage

a. A pile of new debris was doing something.
b. It cluttered up the driveway.
c. In addition, the tenants were gazing at the disgrace.
d. They watched with heavy hearts.

2. *Model:* He stood there, his coat wet, **holding his wet hat,** and said nothing.

Ernest Hemingway, A Farewell to Arms

a. The dog did something.
b. He sat up.
c. His mouth was clenching the rolled newspaper.
d. He was wagging his tail.
e. In addition, he begged a reward.

3. *Model:* The little shack, the rattling, rotting barn were gray-bitten with sea salt, **beaten by the damp wind until they had taken on the color of the granite hills.**

John Steinbeck, "Flight"

a. Something had been done to the upholstered pieces.
b. Something had been done to the expensive, polished tables.
c. They had been moved into the huge dining room.
d. They were covered with endless painter's cloths.
e. This was done so that they would be protected.
f. The protection was from the splattering of paint.

4. *Model:* The strength that had been as a miracle in her body left, and she half-reeled across the floor, **clutching at the back of the chair in which she had spent so many long days staring out over the tin roofs into the main street of Winesburg.**

Sherwood Anderson, Winesburg, Ohio

a. The meeting had been like something.
b. It had been like a marathon among meetings.
c. The meeting continued.
d. In addition, the leader deliberated about his strategy.
e. He was stalling after the last remarks from the representative.
f. The representative was the one with whom he had planned something.
g. What they had planned were so many emergency ploys focusing upon every conceivable tactic.
h. The tactic was for the suppression of the opposition.

PRACTICE 6

The model sentences are arranged in groups according to the position of the participle. Using the structure of the model sentence but your own content, write a sentence imitation for each of the models below. Imitate the structure of the entire sentence, not just the participle phrase.

Sentence Openers

1. **Taking off his cap,** he placed it over the muzzle of his riffle.

Liam O'Flaherty, "The Sniper"

2. **Walking forward, watching the bull's feet,** he saw successively his eyes, his wet muzzle, and the wide, forward-pointing spread of his horns.

Ernest Hemingway, "The Undefeated"

3. **Sitting beside his flowering window while the panes rattled and the wind blew in under the door,** Rosicky gave himself to reflection as he had not done since those Sundays in the loft of the furniture factory in New York, long ago.

Willa Cather, "Neighbor Rosicky"

S-V Splits

4. The turkeys, **roosting in the tree out of coyotes' reach,** clicked drowsily.

John Steinbeck, The Red Pony

5. Her brown face, **upraised,** was stained with tears.

Stephen Crane, The Red Badge of Courage

6. On September 23 the commissioners, **riding in Army ambulances from Fort Robinson and escorted by a somewhat enlarged cavalry troop,** again arrived at the council shelter.

Dee Brown, Bury My Heart at Wounded Knee

Sentence Closers

7. This land was waterless, **furred with the cacti which could store water and with the great-rooted brush which could reach deep into the earth for a little moisture and get along on very little.**

John Steinbeck, The Pearl

8. There was good air and light, and I worked quite hard,

skipping rope, shadow-boxing, doing abdominal exercises lying on the floor in a patch of sunlight that came through the open window, and occasionally scaring the professor when we boxed.

Ernest Hemingway, A Farewell to Arms

9. Nothing else in the world would do but the pure waters which had been summoned from the lakes far away and the sweet fields of grassy dew on early morning, **lifted to the open sky, carried in laundered dusters, nine hundred miles brushed with wind, electrified with high voltage,** and **condensed upon cool air.**

Ray Bradbury, Vintage Bradbury

Multiple Positions

10. She, **thrilled and in part seduced by his words,** instead of resisting as definitely as she would have in any other case, now gazed at him, **fascinated by his enthusiasm.**

Theodore Dreiser, An American Tragedy

11. Al, **bending over the wheel,** kept shifting eyes from the road to the instrument panel, **watching the ammeter needle,** which jerked suspiciously, **watching the oil gauge and the heat indicator.**

John Steinbeck, The Grapes of Wrath

12. **Soiled by the filth of a strange city, spat upon by unknown mouths, driven from the streets into the roadway,** where, a human beast of burden, he pursued his work, **carrying the heaviest loads upon his back, scurrying between carriages, carts, and horses, staring death in the eyes every moment,** he still kept silent.

Isaac Peretz, "Bontsha the Silent"

PRACTICING THE SKILL: SENTENCE COMBINING

PRACTICE 7

In the first sentence in each group, a slash mark (/) indicates that the original sentence has a participle phrase at that place. Combine the sentences underneath into a participle phrase that will fit smoothly into the place indicated by the slash mark. Compare your results with the originals in the References on page 148. Write an imitation of the resulting sentences, using your own content and the structure of the model.

EXAMPLE

a. The little shack, the rattling, rotting barn were gray-bitten with sea salt, / .
b. The shack and the barn were beaten.
c. They were beaten by the damp wind.
d. This happened until they had taken on the color.
e. The color was of the granite hills.

Combination with Participle Phrase

The little shack, the rattling, rotting barn were gray-bitten with sea salt, **beaten by the damp wind until they had taken on the color of the granite hills.**

John Steinbeck, "Flight"

Imitation

The team manager, the surprised, elated team were encouraged, **roused by the roaring fans after the opposing team had fumbled on the fifty-yard line during the last play.**

1a. / , I was wet, cold, and very hungry.
b. I was lying on the floor.
c. The floor was of the flat-car.
d. I was lying with the guns beside me.
e. The guns were under the canvas.

Based on a sentence by Ernest Hemingway, A Farewell to Arms

2a. There was a tattered man, / , who trudged quietly at the youth's side.
b. He was fouled with dust.
c. He was fouled with blood.
d. He was fouled with powder stain.
e. He was fouled from hair to shoes.

Based on a sentence by Stephen Crane, The Red Badge of Courage

3a. I brought the boat up to the stone pier, and the barman pulled in the line, / and / . (two participle phrases)
b. The barman was coiling it.
c. The coiling was on the bottom of the boat.
d. And the barman was hooking the spinner on the edge.
e. The edge was of the gunwale.

Based on a sentence by Ernest Hemingway, A Farewell to Arms

4a. The trail moved up the dry shale hillside, / , / , / . (three participle phrases)
   b. The trail was avoiding rocks.
   c. It was dropping under clefts.
   d. It was climbing in and out of something.
   e. The something was old water scars.

Based on a sentence by John Steinbeck, "Flight"

PRACTICE 8

Combine each list of sentences into one sentence containing a participle phrase. Underline each phrase. You may eliminate words and change their form as long as the intended meaning remains. Punctuate correctly. When you finish, compare your sentences with the originals in the References on page 148.

1a. He was bleeding profusely.
   b. In addition, he was cut off from his supply of eagles' blood.
   c. He had never been closer to death.

Based on a sentence by J. D. Salinger, *Nine Stories*

2a. It happened in an upstairs bedroom.
   b. It happend shortly before dawn.
   c. A young American mother sat.
   d. She sat on the edge of a steel-framed bed.
   e. She was rocking her nursing daughter.

Based on a sentence by Steve Estes, *Called to Die*

3a. By and by, one group after another came straggling back.
   b. They came straggling back to the mouth of the cave.
   c. They were panting.
   d. They were hilarious.
   e. They were smeared from head to foot with tallow drippings.
   f. They were daubed with clay.
   g. In addition, they were entirely delighted with the success of the day.

Based on a sentence by Mark Twain, *The Adventures of Tom Sawyer*

4a. Adolph Knipe took a sip of stout.
   b. He was tasting the malty-bitter flavor.
   c. He was feeling the trickle of cold liquid.
   d. He felt the trickle as it traveled down his throat.
   e. He felt the trickle, in addition, as it settled in the top of his stomach.
   f. At the top of his stomach it was cool at first.
   g. It was then spreading and becoming warm.
   h. It was making a little area of warmness inside him.

Based on a sentence by Roald Dahl, "The Great Automatic Grammatisator"

PRACTICING THE SKILL: SENTENCE EXPANDING

PRACTICE 9

Expand the sentences by adding approximately the same number of words the authors used for their participle phrases. The number is next to the slash mark. To help you start, the beginning words of the participle phrases are provided in **boldface**. Compare your participle phrases with the originals in the References on page 148.

1. With the core of the reel showing, his heart feeling stopped with excitement, /11 **leaning**. . ., Nick thumbed the reel hard with his left hand.

   Ernest Hemingway, "Big Two-Hearted River"

2. Mrs. Carpenter was putting sun-tan oil on Sybil's shoulders, /11 **spreading**. . . .

   J. D. Salinger, Nine Stories

3. Soon the men began to gather, /4 **surveying** . . ., /8 **speaking**. . . .

   Shirley Jackson, "The Lottery"

4. Lil, who would probably be just outside the gate with her boy, would hear Father's voice and hurry in, /8 **knowing** . . ., and almost as soon as she entered the kitchen she would be greeted with a fist or a lifted boot, and soon her rouge and mascara would be mingled with tears and blood as she wilted under a cascade of senseless violence, /7 not **knowing** . . ., /13 **knowing**. . . .

   Christy Brown, Down All the Days

PRACTICE 10

Add a participle phrase to each of the reduced sentences below, blending your content with the rest of the sentence. Each of the sentences in its original, complete version had a participle phrase in the place indicated by the slash mark. When you finish, compare your sentences with the originals in the References on page 149.

Practice a variety of lengths for your participle phrases. Don't be disappointed if your content is unlike that of the original. Try to create content that will work well when blended with the rest of the author's sentence.

1. The children crawled over the shelves and into the potato and onion bins, / .

   Maya Angelou, I Know Why the Caged Bird Sings

2. And he, / , at once looked over his shoulder at her and, / , signaled that he would meet her.

Theodore Dreiser, An American Tragedy

3. In the late afternoon, the truck came back, / and / , there was a layer of dust in the bed, and the hood was covered with dust, and the headlights were obscured with a red flour.

John Steinbeck, The Grapes of Wrath

4. He stood there, / and / , / .

Roald Dahl, "Beware of the Dog"

PRACTICE 11

Revise a piece of your recent writing by expanding selected sentences using participle phrases. Vary the position, length, and number of the phrases.

8

Reviewing and
Applying Professional
Sentence Structures

In the preceding sections of the book, you learned to identify, punctuate, and use three phrases that are frequently used by professional writers but rarely by students. The purpose of this section is to practice using absolute, appositive, and participle phrases in a variety of ways. Repeated practice is necessary for the phrases to become an automatic part of your writing style.

PRACTICE 1

Each sentence below contains an absolute, appositive, or participle phrase. Identify which in each case. Check your answers in the References on page 149.

1. Now, facing the bull, he was conscious of many things at the same time.

    Ernest Hemingway, "The Undefeated"

2. The writer, an old man with a white mustache, had some difficulty in getting into bed.

    Sherwood Anderson, *Winesburg, Ohio*

3. Crouched on the edge of the plateau, the schoolmaster looked at the deserted expanse.

    Albert Camus, *Exile and the Kingdom*

4. His head aching, his throat sore, he forgot to light the cigarette.

    Sinclair Lewis, *Cass Timberlane*

5. He stood quivering, stiff ears forward, eyes rolling so that the whites showed, ...

    John Steinbeck, *The Red Pony*

6. About the bones ants were ebbing away, their pincers full of meat.

Doris Lessing, African Stories

7. I went over and took a teakwood chair with cushions of emerald-green silk, sitting stiffly with my brief case across my knees.

Ralph Ellison, Invisible Man

8. A little house, perched on high piles, appeared black in the distance.

Joseph Conrad, "The Lagoon"

9. One of eleven brothers and sisters, Harriet was a moody, willful child.

Langston Hughes, "Road to Freedom"

10. Buck stood and looked on, the successful champion, the dominant primordial beast who had made his kill and found it good.

Jack London, The Call of the Wild

11. Her gaze, deceiving, transforming her to her imaginings, changed the contour of her sallow-skinned face, re-fashioning her long pointed nose on which a small chilly tear had gathered.

Brian Moore, The Lonely Passion of Judith Hearne

12. Once Enoch Bentley, the older one of the boys, struck his father, old Tom Bentley, with the butt of a teamster's whip, and the old man seemed likely to die.

Sherwood Anderson, Winesburg, Ohio

PRACTICE 2

In the following series of tasks, you'll review absolute, appositive, and participle phrases, noticing their differences, uses, and positions.

Task One

Select a noun. Next to it, write an absolute phrase. Using the same noun, write an appositive phrase. Again using the same noun, write a participle phrase. Put commas before and after the phrases. For example:

1. The handyman, **his tools randomly scattered over the work-bench,** (*absolute*)
2. The handyman, **an elderly, neat gentleman with never a grease stain on his work clothes,** (*appositive*)
3. The handyman, **painting over last year's paint on the old lawn furniture,** (*participle*)

Task Two

Write three sentences, using for part of the content the material you produced in Task One. Add appropriate content to complete each sentence. For example:

1a. The handyman, **his tools randomly scattered over the workbench,** tried to make a little order out of the mess by putting all like things together.

2a. The handyman, **an elderly, neat gentleman with never a grease stain on his work clothes,** told the distraught housewife that in just a few minutes he would have things under control.

3a. The handyman, **painting over last year's paint on the old lawn furniture,** noticed a paint bubble, got out a straight pin, pricked it, scraped the loose paint away, then sanded it smooth.

Task Three

The three phrases can frequently be placed in other positions in relation to the nouns they refer to. To practice moving them, rewrite the sentences from Task Two by placing the phrases in the sentence opener position. In Task Two, they were in the S-V split position. When the phrases are in the sentence opener position, a comma is used after the phrase. For example:

1b. **His tools randomly scattered over the workbench,** the handyman tried to make a little order out of the mess by putting all like things together.

2b **An elderly, neat gentleman with never a grease stain on his work clothes,** the handyman told the distraught housewife that in just a few minutes he would have things under control.

3b. **Painting over last year's paint on the old lawn furniture,** the handyman noticed a paint bubble, got out a straight pin, pricked it, scraped the loose paint away, then sanded it smooth.

Task Four

The phrases may also occur in the sentence closer position. To practice their use in this position, retain the three phrases from the above tasks, but write new content for the rest of each sentence. Place whatever noun you're working with from the preceding tasks immediately before the phrases. When the structures are in the sentence closer position, a comma is used before the phrase. For example:

1c. Mr. Farley, overseer for landscaping and exteriors at Smithton

Estates, criticized the sloppiness of the painter's shed in the maintenance building, and all the while nearby was the handyman, **his tools randomly scattered over the workbench.**

2c. After ruling out the cook, the baby-sitter, and the boy who cut their lawn, they decided that, with their unfortunate fallen financial state, they could only keep in their hire the handyman, **an elderly, neat gentleman with never a grease stain on his work clothes.**

3c. While she was stretching the lace curtains out in the backyard, he was putting old clothes in boxes to give to Goodwill; and paying no attention to either was the handyman, **painting over last year's paint on the old lawn furniture.**

Task Five

Now that you've practiced the three positions in which the phrases may occur, you can work with compounding as a means of improving sentence structure through use of these three phrases. Compounding adds one or more like phrases to a sentence.

Select one of your sentences containing an absolute phrase and add another absolute phrase. Do the same with the appositive and participle phrases. For example:

1d. The handyman, **his tools randomly scattered over the workbench, his hands moving determinedly,** tried to make a little order out of the mess by putting all like things together.

2d. After ruling out the cook, the baby-sitter, and the boy who cut their lawn, they decided that, with their unfortunate fallen financial state, they could only keep in their hire the handyman, **an elderly, neat gentleman with never a grease stain on his work clothes, a man in their employ for over two generations.**

3d. The handyman, **painting over last year's paint on the old lawn furniture, acting upon his reputation as a perfectionist,** noticed a paint bubble, got out a straight pin, pricked it, scraped the loose paint away, then sanded it smooth.

PRACTICE 3

To review the three phrases, the positions in which they may occur, and the methods by which they may be compounded, do the following. For each worker listed, write a sentence of at least 20 words describing the worker on the job. Include, underline, and punctuate the required phrase described in parentheses.

1. BARTENDER (sentence opener absolute)
2. JOCKEY (S-V split absolute)
3. NEWSPAPER BOY (sentence closer absolute)
4. BANK TELLER (sentence opener appositive)
5. BABY-SITTER (S-V split appositive)
6. FIREMAN (sentence closer appositive)
7. ACTOR (sentence opener participle)
8. MODEL (S-V split participle)
9. TAXI DRIVER (sentence closer participle)
10. CASHIER AT A SUPERMARKET (sentence opener compound absolutes)
11. SECRETARY (S-V split compound absolutes)
12. TEACHER (sentence closer compound absolutes)
13. DANCER (sentence opener compound appositives)
14. WRITER (S-V split compound appositives)
15. TRUCK DRIVER (sentence closer compound appositives)
16. DETECTIVE (sentence opener compound participles)
17. SALESPERSON (S-V split compound participles)
18. WAITRESS (sentence closer compound participles)
19. ARTIST (one of each—absolute, appositive, and participle—in any order, in any position)

PRACTICE 4

The list of sentences below illustrates the combination of phrases (absolutes, appositives, participles) within a sentence. Combinations are common in professional writing and worth using wisely in your own.

Identify the type of phrases in **boldface**. Check your answers in the References on page 150. Next, write six imitations, using any two models you choose from each group of sentence lengths—short, medium, long. For your six sentences, imitate the structure and length of the models but use your own content.

Short Sentences

1. **Gasping, his hands raw,** he reached a flat place at the top.

   Richard Connell, "The Most Dangerous Game"

2. He stood there, **his coat wet, holding his wet hat,** and said nothing.

   Ernest Hemingway, A Farewell to Arms

3. He stood quivering, **stiff ears forward, eyes rolling so that the whites showed, pretending to be frightened.**

   John Steinbeck, The Red Pony

4. He walked in the rain, **an old man with his hat off, a carabinieri on either side.**

Ernest Hemingway, A Farewell to Arms

Medium Sentences

5. **One of many small groups of children, each child carrying his little bag of crackling,** we trod the long road home in the cold winter afternoon.

Peter Abrahams, Tell Freedom

6. It ran, **its pelvic bones crushing aside trees and bushes, its taloned feet clawing damp earth, leaving prints six inches deep wherever it settled its weight.**

Ray Bradbury, A Sound of Thunder

7. I turned to "Annabel Lee," and we walked up and down the garden rows, **the cool dirt between our toes, reciting the beautifully sad lines.**

Maya Angelou, I Know Why the Caged Bird Sings

8. The masters were in their places for the first Chapel, **seated in stalls in front of and at right angles to us, suggesting by their worn expressions and careless postures that they had never been away at all.**

John Knowles, A Separate Peace

Long Sentences

9. The midwife, **arriving late,** had found the baby's head pulled out of shape, **its neck stretched, its body warped;** and she had pushed the head back and molded the body with her hands.

John Steinbeck, Grapes of Wrath

10. He trembled alone there in the middle of the park for hours, **wondering what would happen if he had an attack of appendicitis, unnerved by the thoughts of a fainting spell, horrified by the realization that he might have to move his bowels,** until at last we came.

John Knowles, A Separate Peace

11. Out in the distances the fans of windmills twinkled, **turning,** and about the base of each, about the drink tank, was a speckle of dark dots, **a gather of cattle grazing in moonlight and meditating upon good grass, block salt, impermanence, and love.**

Glendon Swarthout, Bless the Beasts and Children

12. The day my son Laurie started kindergarden he renounced corduroy overalls with bibs and began wearing blue jeans with a belt; I watched him go off the first morning with the older girl next door, **seeing clearly that an era of my life was ended, my sweet-voiced nursery-school tot replaced by a long-trousered, swaggering character who forgot to stop at the corner and wave good-bye to me.**

Shirley Jackson, "Charles"

PRACTICE 5

Add sentences to the professional paragraphs below. The kind of sentence to add is described. The first part of the description is the suggested length for your sentence, based on the length of the deleted sentence:

Short: 1–15 words
Medium: 16–30 words
Long: 31–50 words

The second part of the description is the content, and the third part is the type of phrase (absolute, appositive, participle) to include within your sentence. When you finish, compare your sentences with the originals in the References on page 150.

There's no way you can duplicate the author's sentences, nor should you. The purpose of the Practice is to compose well-written sentences that blend well with those of the authors.

1. From *Ethan Frome* by Edith Wharton, a paragraph describing a cat knocking over and breaking a valuable dish:

The cat, unnoticed, had crept up on muffled paws from Zeena's seat to the table, and was stealthily elongating its body in the direction of the milk-jug, which stood between Ethan and Mattie. The two leaned forward at the same moment, and their hands met on the handle of the jug. Mattie's hand was underneath, and Ethan kept his clasped on it a moment longer than was necessary. [INSERT— LENGTH: *medium*; TOPIC: *the cat breaking the dish*; PHRASE: *one participle.*]

2. From *The Red Badge of Courage* by Stephen Crane, a paragraph describing a dead soldier:

He was being looked at by a dead man who was seated with his back against a columnlike tree. The corpse was dressed in a uniform that once had been blue, but was now faded to a melancholy shade of green. [INSERT—LENGTH: *medium*; TOPIC: *the eyes of the corpse*; PHRASE: *one participle.*] The mouth was open. Its red had changed to an appalling yellow. Over the gray skin of the face ran little ants. One was trundling some sort of a bundle along the lower lip.

3. From *Call It Sleep* by Henry Roth, a paragraph narrating a child spilling soup:

He dared not refuse, though the very thought of eating sickened him. [INSERT—LENGTH: *medium*; TOPIC: *attempting to eat the first spoonful*; PHRASE: *one participle*.] Instead of reaching his mouth, the spoon reached only his chin, struck against the hollow under his lower lip, scalded it, fell from his nerveless fingers into the plate. [INSERT—LENGTH: *short*; TOPIC: *soup splashing on his clothing and table cloth*; PHRASES: *series of two participles*.] With a feeling of terror David watched the crimson splotches on the cloth widen till they met each other.

4. From "All-Gold Cañon" by Jack London, a paragraph narrating the shooting of a gold miner:

While he debated, a loud, crashing noise burst on his ear. At the same instant he received a stunning blow on the left side of the back, and from the point of impact felt a rush of flame through his flesh. He sprang up in the air, but halfway to his feet collapsed. [INSERT—LENGTH: *long*; TOPIC: *the miner falling to the ground*; PHRASES: *series of three absolutes*.] His legs twitched convulsively several times. His body was shaken as with a mighty ague. There was a slow expansion of the lungs, accompanied by a deep sigh. Then the air was slowly, very slowly, exhaled, and his body as slowly flattened itself down into inertness.

5. From *Winesburg, Ohio* by Sherwood Anderson, a paragraph explaining an adolescent's philosophy of life:

There is a time in the life of every boy when he for the first time takes the backward view of life. Perhaps that is the moment when he crosses the line into manhood. The boy is walking through the streets of his town. He is thinking of the future and of the figure he will cut in the world. Ambitions and regrets awake within him. Suddenly something happens; he stops under a tree and waits as for a voice calling his name. Ghosts of old things creep into his consciousness; the voices outside of himself whisper a message concerning the limitations of life. From being quite sure of himself and his future he becomes not at all sure. If he be an imaginative boy, a door is torn open and for the first time he looks upon the world, seeing, as though they marched in procession before him, the countless figures of men who before his time have come out of nothingness into the world, lived their lives and again disappeared into nothingness. The sadness of sophistication has come to the boy. With a little gasp he sees himself as merely a leaf blown by the wind through the streets of his village. [INSERT—LENGTH: *long*; TOPIC: *the inevitability of death*; PHRASES: series of two appositives.] He shivers and looks eagerly about. [INSERT—LENGTH: *medium*; TOPIC: the shortness of life; PHRASE: one appositive.] Already he hears death calling. With all his heart he wants to come close to some other human, touch someone with his hands, be touched by the hand of another. If he prefers that the other be a woman, that is because he believes that a woman will be gentle, that she will understand. He wants, most of all, understanding.

III

Achieving Professional
Sentence Variety

This part of the textbook teaches how professional writers fill three slots in their sentences to achieve sentence variety: the beginning, or sentence openers; the slot between a subject and its verb, or S-V splits; and the ending, or sentence closers. The use of these three positions is common in professional writing, rare in student writing.

In learning to imitate the sentence structures frequently used by professional writers but only rarely by students, you can greatly increase the quality of the sentences you compose and also of the paragraphs containing those sentences.

Throughout this part of the textbook you'll study sentence variety through the four techniques you've been using:

SENTENCE SCRAMBLING
SENTENCE IMITATING
SENTENCE COMBINING
SENTENCE EXPANDING

All four rely upon sentences written by professional writers. Through frequent practice of the techniques, you'll produce sentences that closely resemble in structure and variety those written by professionals.

9

Sentence Openers

IDENTIFYING THE SKILL

Here's a list of sentences, all written by professional writers, but with some parts deleted.

1. The outlook was anything but bright.
2. No more than six or seven were out on the cold, open platform.
3. He started along the main corridor on his way toward the stairs.
4. Manuel noticed the points of the bull's horns.
5. Elizabeth Willard lighted a lamp and put it on a dressing table that stood by the door.

Now compare the sentences above with the originals below. Notice that it's the **boldface** parts (sentence openers) that account for the professional sentence variety.

1a. **With the newcomers hopeless and forlorn, and the old team worn out by twenty-five hundred miles of continuous trail,** the outlook was anything but bright.

Jack London, *The Call of the Wild*

2a. **Of the twenty-some young men who were waiting at the station for their dates to arrive on the ten-fifty-two,** no more than six or seven were out on the cold, open platform.

J. D. Salinger, *Franny and Zooey*

3a. **With the blood specimen in his left hand, walking in a kind of distraction that he had felt all morning, probably because of the dream and his restless night,** he started along the main corridor on his way toward the stairs.

John Hersey, *Hiroshima*

4a. **Standing still now and spreading the red cloth of the muleta with the sword, pricking the point into the cloth so that the sword, now held in his left hand, spread the red flannel like the jib of a boat,** Manuel noticed the points of the bull's horns.

Ernest Hemingway, "The Undefeated"

5a. **In her room, tucked away in a corner of the old Willard House,** Elizabeth Willard lighted a lamp and put it on a dressing table that stood by the door.

Sherwood Anderson, Winesburg, Ohio

CHARACTERISTICS OF A SENTENCE OPENER

Definition

A sentence opener is any structure or combination of structures that occupies the introductory position of a sentence. Here are examples:

1. **Alone,** I would often speak to her. . . .

Henry Miller, Stand Still Like a Humingbird

2. **Milky and opaque,** it has the pinkish bloom of the sky. . . .

Anne Morrow Lindbergh, Gift from the Sea

3. **At the gate,** I show the pass to a young Japanese private. . . .

Richard E. Kim, Lost Names

4. **On Monday afternoons, when we are allowed to have visitors,** the tent is packed with parents and relatives. . . .

Richard E. Kim, Lost Names

5. **Suffering, sick, and angry, but also grimly satisfied with his new stoicism,** he stood there leaning on his rifle. . . .

Doris Lessing, African Stories

Punctuation

In addition to any punctuation required within the sentence opener itself, a comma is placed after it.

PRACTICING THE SKILL: SENTENCE SCRAMBLING

PRACTICE 1

Unscramble the sentence parts to produce a sentence with a sentence opener. Some sentences have more than one sentence opener; for those, decide the best order. Punctuate correctly, with a comma following each sentence opener. Compare your results with the professional writers' sentences in the References on page 150. Decide whether yours are as effectively organized as the professional writers'.

1a. tipping backward again
 b. drifting into sleep

   c. into memory
   d. he lost his balance

Judith Guest, Ordinary People

2a. of paper
   b. without a word
   c. she takes a piece
   d. out of her pants pocket.

Richard E. Kim, Lost Names

3a. but the most innocent pleasure
   b. even then
   c. our shyness prevented us from sharing anything
   d. when we might have kissed and embraced unrestrainedly.

Henry Miller, Stand Still Like a Hummingbird

4a. I heard their laughter crackling and popping
   b. in a cooking stove
   c. before the girls got to the porch
   d. like pine logs

Maya Angelou, I Know Why the Caged Bird Sings

5a. said something about letting me go on in her place
   b. having seen me perform before Mother's friends
   c. she was very upset
   d. when she came into the wings
   e. and argued with the stage manager who

Charles Spencer Chaplin (Charlie Chaplan), My Autobiography

6a. and her children
   b. being a star in her own right
   c. she was well able
   d. earning twenty-five pounds a week
   e. to support herself

Charles Spencer Chaplin (Charlie Chaplin), My Autobiography

7a. facing the bull
   b. at the same time
   c. he was conscious
   d. now
   e. of many things

Ernest Hemingway, "The Undefeated"

8a. but like something he had never even imagined
   b. was a figure from a dream
   c. there
   d. a strange beast that was horned and drunken-legged
   e. between two trees
   f. against a background of gaunt black rocks

Doris Lessing, "A Sunrise on the Veld"

PRACTICE 2

Each sentence below is a slightly scrambled version of a professional writer's sentence. In the original version, there's a sentence opener. The scrambled version, however, has moved the sentence opener out of the introductory position. Identify any structures that could become sentence openers and rearrange each sentence so that it has a sentence opener. Compare yours with the originals in the References on page 151. Which are better? Why?

Scrambled Sentences

1. My turn came at last, after what seemed hours.

   Peter Abrahams, *Tell Freedom*

2. Other children trotted in twos and threes, behind and in front of us.

   Peter Abrahams, *Tell Freedom*

3. Everything was perfect, even the punctuation, on the very next try a few days later.

   Roald Dahl, "The Great Automatic Grammatisator"

4. He had persuaded something like seventy per cent of the writers on his list to sign the contract in the end, after several months of work.

   Roald Dahl, "The Great Automatic Grammatisator"

5. A fat little old man walked nervously up and down upon the half decayed veranda of a small frame house that stood near the edge of a ravine near the town of Winesburg, Ohio.

   Sherwood Anderson, *Winesburg, Ohio*

6. He stood there leaning on his rifle, and watched the seething black mound grow smaller, suffering, sick, and angry, but also grimly satisfied with his new stoicism.

   Doris Lessing, "A Sunrise on the Veld"

PRACTICING THE SKILL: SENTENCE IMITATING

PRACTICE 3

Underneath the model sentence below are two imitations. The imitations are presented as a list of scrambled sentence parts for you to unscramble to duplicate the structure of the model. Unscramble each sentence to produce a sentence similar in structure to the model. Compare yours with the ones in the References on page 151.

The model sentence contains *two* sentence openers, one in the introductory position for each of the two main clauses in the sentence. The sentence openers are in **boldface**.

Model

In the city, when the word came to him, he walked about at night through the streets thinking of the matter, and **when he had come home and had got the work on the farm well under way,** he went again at night to walk through the forests and over the low hills and to think of God.

Sherwood Anderson, Winesburg, Ohio

Scrambled Imitations

1a. they emptied it out in minutes piling up the garbage
 b. and to shift with thuds
 c. at the dumpster
 d. and as they pulled away and started the turn near Canal Street much too fast
 e. when the truck arrived with junk
 f. the remaining debris began to clank in the back and near the cabin

2a. from the start
 b. he dragged himself at eight o'clock to open up the store and the prepayment office
 c. because the store had opened with haste
 d. and because he had been up late last night and had the alarm in the morning set too late
 e. Jackson pondered constantly in dread during the day wondering about his boss
 f. and to worry over his possible punishment

PRACTICE 4

First, read the model several times, paying special attention to the structure of the sentence. In each model, the sentence opener is in **boldface**. Study it. Also, study the rest of the sentence carefully; you'll need to be familiar with not only the sentence opener but also the rest of the sentence structure.

Next, read the list of sentences underneath the model. Combine these into one sentence having the same (or similar) sentence structure as the model. Compare your sentences with the ones in the References on page 152.

Finally, write an imitation of the model, keeping the same structure as the model but providing your own content.

EXAMPLE

Model

About a year later, when I had returned from the West, sadder and wiser, to return to the arms of "the widow" from whom I had run away, we met again by chance.

Henry Miller, Stand Still Like a Hummingbird

Sentences to Be Combined

a. It occurred almost an hour ago.
b. I was mowing the lawn then.
c. I was tired and dirty.
d. The mowing of the lawn was to spruce up the appearance of the property.
e. I had heavily invested in the property.
f. The real estate agent arrived with the house-hunters.

Combination

Almost an hour ago, as I was mowing the lawn, tired and dirty, to spruce up the appearance of the property in which I had heavily invested, the real estate agent arrived with the house-hunters.

Imitation

Around the same time, when he had wrapped the manuscript, weary but satisfied, to mail it to the editor with whom he had discussed revisions, he talked twice with the advertising director.

---

1. *Model:* **While touring with this company,** she met and ran off with the middle-aged lord to Africa.

Charles Spencer Chaplin (Charlie Chaplin), My Autobiography

   a. This incident occurred after a meeting.
   b. The meeting was with the President.
   c. He signed the letter after meeting with the President.
   d. He delivered the letter.
   e. The person to whom he delivered it was the secretary.

2. *Model:* **When I came back in the store,** I took Momma's hand, and we both walked outside to look at the pattern.

Maya Angelou, I Know Why the Caged Bird Sings

a. It happened after she tried something.
b. What she tried was the choreography.
c. She met the director.
d. In addition, they planned to confer with someone.
e. The person they planned to confer with was the producer.

3. *Model:* **In all the mornings and evenings of the winter months,** young and old, big and small, were helpless victims of the bitter cold.

Peter Abrahams, Tell Freedom

a. It happened through all the ups of the trial.
b. Also, it happened through all the downs of the trial.
c. The lawyers and the judge had done something.
d. Also, the defendant and the jury had done something.
e. All of them had been listeners.
f. Their listening was intense.
g. What they listened to was the expert testimony.

4. *Model:* **Too tired to help the bush boy with fire-making, and too worn-out to eat,** he crawled wearily across his sister, put his head on her lap, and fell instantly asleep.

James V. Marshall, Walkabout

a. Miss Simpson was too pleasant to fight.
b. The fight would have been with the customer.
c. The fight would have been about the return.
d. In addition, Miss Simpson was too agreeable to resist.
e. Miss Simpson agreed with a smile.
f. She refunded the money without protest.
g. Also, she remained remarkably calm.

PRACTICE 5

Following the structure of the model sentence, but using your own content, write a sentence imitation for each of the models below. Imitate the structure of the entire sentence, not just the sentence opener.

1. **In all the years which have since elapsed,** she remains the woman I loved and lost, the unattainable one.

Henry Miller, Stand Still Like a Hummingbird

2. **When we had made our way downstairs,** we saw the woman with the lovely complexion, Miss Pilzer, screaming and begging to be allowed to go with her mother.

Gerda Weissmann Klein, All But My Life

3. **Often, walking home at night, after having made a tour of**

her house, I would yell her name aloud, imploringly, as if to beg her to grant me the favour of an audience from on high.

Henry Miller, Stand Still Like a Hummingbird

4. **Never having enjoyed, to any considerable extent, her soothing presence, her tender and watchful care,** I received the tidings of her death with much the same emotions I should have probably felt at the death of a stranger.

Frederick Douglass, "A Slave's Beginning"

5. **In my robe and barefoot in the backyard, under cover of going to see about my new beans,** I gave myself up to the gentle warmth and thanked God that no matter what evil I had done in my life He had allowed me to live to see this day.

Maya Angelou, I Know Why the Caged Bird Sings

6. **Like a boil that can never be cured so long as it is covered up but must be opened with all its ugliness to the natural medicines of air and light,** injustice must be exposed, with all the tension its exposure creates, to the light of human conscience and the air of natural opinion before it can be cured.

Martin Luther King, Jr., "Letter from Birmingham Jail"

PRACTICING THE SKILL: SENTENCE COMBINING

PRACTICE 6

In the first sentence in each group, a slash mark (/) indicates that the original sentence has a sentence opener. Convert the sentence underneath into a sentence opener that will fit smoothly into the place indicated by the slash mark. Compare your sentences with the originals in the References on page 152.

After you've combined the sentences into one, write an imitation of the resulting sentence, using your own content but the structure of the model.

EXAMPLE

a. /, Doctor Parcival began to walk up and down in the office of the *Winesburg Eagle*, where George Willard sat listening.

b. Doctor Parcival was jumping to his feet and breaking off the tale.

Combination with Sentence Openers

Jumping to his feet and breaking off the tale, Doctor Parcival began to walk up and down in the office of the *Winesburg Eagle*, where George Willard sat listening.

Sherwood Anderson, *Winesburg, Ohio*

Imitation

Gaining on the front-runner and pulling out all the stops, number thirteen started to swing wide from the rest of the horses, where the track was sloppier.

1a. / , the manuscript had been read and accepted by an enthusiastic publisher.
   b. This happened within a week.

Based on a sentence by Roald Dahl, "The Great Automatic Grammatisator"

2a. /, the German submarines arrived in the middle of the night.
   b. The submarines were like silent, hungry sharks that swim in the darkness of the sea.

Based on a sentence by Theodore Taylor, "The Cay"

3a. /, Rosicky gave himself to reflection as he had not done since those Sundays in the loft of the furniture factory in New York, long ago.
   b. Rosicky was sitting beside his flowering window while the panes rattled and the wind blew in under the door.

Based on a sentence by Willa Cather, "Neighbor Rosicky"

4a. /, the schoolmaster looked at the deserted expanse.
   b. The schoolmaster was crouched on the edge of the plateau.

Based on a sentence by Albert Camus, "The Guest"

5a. /, /, /, he felt as if he could squeal or laugh out loud.
   b. And then something happened.
   c. His feet were sinking in the soft nap of the carpet.
   d. His hand was in one pocket clutching the money.

Based on a sentence by Theodore Dreiser, *An American Tragedy*

6a. /, /, /, /, /, /, he still kept silent.
   b. He was soiled by the filth of a strange city.
   c. He was spat upon by unknown mouths.
   d. He was driven from the streets into the roadway.
   e. He was carrying the heaviest loads upon his back.
   f. He was scurrying between carriages, carts, and horses.
   g. He was staring death in the eyes every moment.

Based on a sentence by Isaac Peretz, "Bontsha the Silent"

PRACTICE 7

Combine each list of sentences into one sentence containing a sentence opener(s). Underline the part of the resulting sentence that is the sentence opener(s). You may eliminate words, or change their form, so long as the intended meaning remains. Punctuate correctly. When you finish, compare your work with the professional writers' sentences in the References on page 152.

1a. Something happens when a man remains single.
   b. He converts himself into a temptation.
   c. The temptation is permanent.
   d. The temptation is public.

Based on a sentence by Oscar Wilde

2a. Pain was shooting.
   b. It was shooting up my entire arm.
   c. I lay panting.
   d. I panted on the edge of the pool.
   e. In addition, I gingerly began to feel my wrist.

Based on a sentence by Theodore Taylor, "The Cay"

3a. Gumbril was pretending to take an interest.
   b. The interest was in the New Season's Models.
   c. Gumbril was squinting sideways over the burning tip of his cigar.
   d. While doing these things, he made an inventory.
   e. The inventory was of her features.

Based on a sentence by Aldous Huxley, *Antic Hay*

4a. It happened in the frosty December dusk.
   b. Their cabins looked neat and snug with pale blue smoke rising.
   c. It was rising from the chimneys.
   d. Their cabins looked neat and snug with doorways glowing.
   e. The doorways were glowing amber from the fires inside.

Based on a sentence by Harper Lee, *To Kill a Mockingbird*

5a. It happened in the darkness.
   b. The darkness was in the hallway.
   c. The hallway was by the door.
   d. The sick woman arose.
   e. In addition, the sick woman started again toward her own room.

Based on a sentence by Sherwood Anderson, *Winesburg, Ohio*

6a. It happened in her girlhood.
   b. It happened also before her marriage.
   c. Her marriage was with Tom Willard.
   d. What happened is that Elizabeth had borne a somewhat shaky reputation.
   e. The reputation was in Winesburg.

Based on a sentence by Sherwood Anderson, *Winesburg, Ohio*

7a. It happened near the edge of town.

  b. What happened was that the group had to walk around an automobile.

  c. The automobile was burned and squatting on the narrow road.

  d. In addition, the bearers on one side fell.

  e. They were unable to see their way in the darkness.

  f. They fell into a deep ditch.

Based on a sentence by John Hersey, Hiroshima

8a. It happened by nightfall of an average courting day.

  b. A certain kind of fiddler crab then was in pretty sad shape.

  c. The certain kind is one who has been standing on tiptoe.

  d. The standing took place for eight or ten hours.

  e. While standing, it was waving a heavy claw.

  f. The waving was in the air.

Based on a sentence by James Thurber, "Courtship Through the Ages"

PRACTICING THE SKILL SENTENCE EXPANDING

PRACTICE 8

Add appropriate sentence openers to each of the reduced sentences below. Each of the sentences, in their complete versions, has sentence openers in the places indicated by slash marks. When you finish, compare your sentences with the originals in the References on page 153.

EXAMPLE

Reduced Sentence: /, /, Tarzan took to the trees in search of game.
Student-Expanded Sentence: **With Jane and Boy to provide for now, both hungry after their ordeal with the hostile tribe,** Tarzan took to the trees in search of game.
Original Sentence: **Later in the day, his rope repaired,** Tarzan took to the trees in search of game.

Edgar Rice Burroughs, "Tarzan's First Love"

---

1. /, he sat down on the edge of the couch, sat for hours without moving.

Willa Cather, "Coming, Aphrodite!"

2. /, she had many beaux, but these small-town boys didn't interest her.

Willa Cather, "Coming, Aphrodite!"

3. /, the tall dark girl had been in those days much confused.

Sherwood Anderson, Winesburg, Ohio

4. /, /, an invitation out meant an evening in other people's lives, and therefore freedom from his own, and it meant the possibility of laughter that would surprise him—how good it was to be alive and healthy, to have a body that had not given up in spite of everything.

Joyce Carol Oates, "The Wheel of Love"

5. /, the truck came back, bumping and rattling through the dust, and there was a layer of dust in the bed, and the hood was covered with dust, and the headlights were obscured with a red flour.

John Steinbeck, The Grapes of Wrath

6. /, they threaded the shimmering channel in the rowboat and, tying it to a jutting rock, began climbing the cliff together.

F. Scott Fitzgerald, Flappers and Philosophers

7. /, /, she would still keep her eyes closed for a long time, then open them and relish with astonishment the blue of the brand-new curtains, replacing the apricot-pink which had filtered the morning light into the room where she had slept as a girl.

Colette, "The Hand"

8. /, /, /, Dr. Sasaki lost all sense of profession and stopped working as a skillful surgeon and a sympathetic man; he became an automaton, mechanically wiping, daubing, winding, wiping, daubing, winding.

John Hersey, Hiroshima

PRACTICE 9

Eight out of the ten sentences in the following student-written paragraph begin in a very basic way: the main clause with no sentence opener preceding it. The purpose of this Practice is to improve the paragraph by adding sentence openers to some of the student's sentences.

First, identify which eight sentences do not have sentence openers. Next, choosing any *three* of those sentences, provide sentence openers for each.

EXAMPLE

Original Sentence

The nurse had helped him to lie down and had given him a sedative.

Revision with Sentence Opener

After several hours in the recovery room, when, still groggy, he was wheeled back to his room, the nurse had helped him to lie down and had given him a sedative.

Paragraph for Revision

1. The nurse, walking down the corridor and humming a pleasant tune, turned into the small room. 2. Sitting on the bed was the old man, weak and pale from his lingering illness. 3. The nurse, a middle-aged, attractive woman and a no-nonsense professional, tried to comfort the old man. 4. She spoke to him, but he could not hear her. 5. The operation which had spared his life had taken away his hearing. 6. After several hours in the recovery room, when, still groggy, he was wheeled back to his room, the nurse had helped him to lie down and had given him a sedative. 7. She checked the room to see how he was. 8. She left the room to see about his medication but came back in only a few minutes. 9. She looked at him sitting there on the bed, his eyelids slowly falling and his mind drifting off into silent sleep. 10. She liked him immensely, for his courage, for his expressive face, which reminded her of her grandfather's when she was a little girl.

PRACTICE 10

From a recent piece of writing of your own, select five sentences that do not begin with sentence openers. Add them.

10

S-V Splits

IDENTIFYING THE SKILL

Here's a list of sentences, all written by well-known writers, but with some parts deleted. The subject and the verb are indicated.

1. Her hair made an ash-blond crown.
<small>s   v</small>

2. The all-powerful auto industry was suddenly forced to *listen* for a change.

3. Their restless activity had given him his name.

4. Henry Strader made the same joke every morning.

5. The coming of industrialism has worked a tremendous change in the lives and in the habits of thought of our people of Mid-America.

Now compare the sentences above with the originals below. Notice that it's the **boldface** parts (S-V splits) that account for the professional sentence variety.

1a. Her hair, **braided and wrapped around her head,** made an ash-blond crown.

John Steinbeck, The Grapes of Wrath

2a. The all-powerful auto industry, **accustomed to telling the customer what sort of car he wanted,** was suddenly forced to *listen* for a change.

Jessica Mitford, The American Way of Death

3a. Their restless activity, **like unto the beating of the wings of an imprisoned bird,** had given him his name.

Sherwood Anderson, Winesburg, Ohio

4a. Henry Strader, **an old man who had been on the farm since Jesse came into possession and who before David's time had never been known to make a joke,** made the same joke every morning.

Sherwood Anderson, *Winesburg, Ohio*

5a. The coming of industrialism, **attended by all the roar and rattle of affairs, the shrill cries of millions of new voices that have come among us from overseas, the going and coming of trains, the growth of cities, the building of the inter-urban car lines that weave in and out of towns and past farm-houses, and now in these days the coming of automobiles,** has worked a tremendous change in the lives and in the habits of thought of our people of Mid-America.

Sherwood Anderson, *Winesburg, Ohio*

CHARACTERISTICS OF AN S-V SPLIT

Definition

An S-V split is any structure or combination of structures that occupies the position between the subject and the verb of a sentence. Here are examples:

1. A sigh, **short and faint,** marked an almost imperceptible pause, and then his words flowed on, without a stir, without a gesture.

Joseph Conrad, "The Lagoon"

2. Poppa, **a good quiet man,** spent the last hours before our parting moving aimlessly about the yard, keeping to himself and avoiding me.

Gordon Parks, "My Mother's Dream for Me"

3. The Russians, **coming from streets around the cemetery,** were hurrying, singly or in groups, in the spring snow in the direction of the caves in the ravine, some running in the middle of the slushy cobblestone streets.

Bernard Malamud, *The Fixer*

4. The twins, **smeary in the face, eating steadily from untidy paper sacks of sweets,** followed them in a detached way.

Katherine Anne Porter, *Ship of Fools*

5. This leader, **whose word was law among boys who defied authority for the sake of defiance,** was no more than twelve or thirteen years old and looked even younger.

Henry G. Felsen, "Horatio"

Punctuation

In addition to any punctuation required within the S-V split, place a comma before and after the split.

PRACTICING THE SKILL: SENTENCE SCRAMBLING

PRACTICE 1

Unscramble the sentence parts to produce a sentence with an S-V split. Punctuate correctly, with one comma before the S-V split and one after. Compare your results with the professional writers' sentences in the References on page 154.

1a. in getting into bed
 b. the writer
 c. had some difficulty
 d. an old man with a white mustache

Sherwood Anderson, *Winesburg, Ohio*

2a. suddenly arose and advanced toward him
 b. absorbed in his own idea
 c. his terror grew until his whole body shook
 d. when Jesse Bentley

Sherwood Anderson, *Winesburg, Ohio*

3a. the twins
 b. in a detached way
 c. smeary in the face, eating steadily from untidy paper sacks of sweets
 d. followed them

Katherine Anne Porter, *Ship of Fools*

4a. the sinuous, limbless body
 b. his hands
 c. ran up and down the soft-skinned baby body
 d. beyond control

Judith Merrill, "That Only a Mother"

5a. one of them
 b. talked continually
 c. a slender young man with white hands, the son of a jeweler in Winesburg
 d. of virginity

Sherwood Anderson, *Winesburg, Ohio*

6a. felt more pleasure than pain
b. fresh from the pounding of Johnnie's fists
c. his face
d. and the driving snow
e. in the wind

Stephen Crane, "The Blue Hotel"

7a. with the knotted, cracked joints and the square, horn-thick nails
b. the big hands
c. of a shed after work
d. hang loose off the wrist bone
e. on the wall
f. like clumsy, homemade tools

Robert Penn Warren, "The Patented Gate and the Mean Hamburger"

8a. who had brought flowers and baskets of fruit
b. took leisurely leave
c. their thin dark hair sleeked down over their ears, their thin-soled black slippers too short in the toes and badly run over at high heels
d. of a half dozen local young men
e. the four pretty, slatternly Spanish girls
f. with kisses all around

Katherine Anne Porter, Ship of Fools

PRACTICING THE SKILL: SENTENCE IMITATING

PRACTICE 2

Underneath the model sentences are two imitations, presented as a list of scrambled sentence parts for you to unscramble to duplicate the structure of the model. Unscramble each sentence to produce a sentence similar in structure to the model. Compare yours with the ones in the References on page 154. The model contains *two* S-V splits, one in each of the two main clauses. The S-V splits are in **boldface.**

Model

In the presence of George Willard, Wing Biddlebaum, **who for twenty years had been the town mystery,** lost something of his timidity; and his shadowy personality, **submerged in a sea of doubts,** came forth to look at the world.

Sherwood Anderson, Winesburg, Ohio

Scrambled Imitations

1a. warned the traffic to make way
 b. in the flurry of traffic
 c. who only an hour ago had been asleep
 d. wailing like a giant in agony
 e. the ambulance driver
 f. and his siren
 g. gripped the steering wheel

2a. derived from his year's self-control with alcohol
 b. near the field of wheat
 c. who a year ago had been an irresponsible drunk
 d. tough-skinned Jasper
 e. allowed him to concentrate on farming
 f. and his serenity
 g. walked peacefully among his crops

PRACTICE 3

First, read the model several times, paying special attention to the structure of the sentence. In each model the S-V split is in **boldface** type. Study it. Also, study the rest of the sentence carefully: you'll need to be familiar with not only the S-V split but also the rest of the sentence structure.

Next, read the list of sentences underneath the model. Combine these into one sentence having the same (or similar) sentence structure as the model. Compare your sentences with the ones in the References on page 155.

Finally, write an imitation of the model, keeping the same sentence structure as the model but providing your own content.

EXAMPLE

Model

At daybreak Rainsford, **lying near the swamp,** was awakened by a sound that made him know that he had new things to learn about fear.

Richard Connell, "The Most Dangerous Game"

Sentences to Be Combined

a. It occurred before the game.
 b. Winston was the one to whom it happened.
 c. He was suffering from nervousness.

d. Winston was telephoned.

e. A fellow player called him.

f. The player told him something.

g. What he told Winston was that Winston had several plays.

h. The plays Winston had to revise.

i. The revision had to take place before the game.

Combination

Before the game Winston, **suffering from nervousness,** was telephoned by a fellow player who told him that Winston had several plays to revise before the game.

Imitation

Near the junkyard Mr. Pauley, **jogging through the intersection,** was surprised by a truck which made him realize that he should change his route to arrive after dawn.

---

1. *Model:* Van'ka Zhukov, **a boy of nine who had been apprenticed to the shoemaker Alyakhin three months ago,** was staying up that Christmas eve.

   Anton Chekhov, "Van'ka"

   a. Nielsen Rating Service was in operation.

   b. This service is a determiner of TV ratings.

   c. The ratings had been accepted by the TV networks that season.

   d. The operation the service was engaged in was surveying this morning.

2. *Model:* Dvoira, **the dark-uddered cow,** was out in the field behind the hut, browsing under a leafless poplar tree, and Yakov went out to her.

   Bernard Malamud, *The Fixer*

   a. The cook was concerned about something.

   b. He was a fine-bellied gourmet.

   c. He was back in the kitchen at the closet freezer.

   d. There, he was ruminating about the latest beef selections.

   e. In addition, the butcher reassured him.

3. *Model:* When his father, **who was old and twisted with toil,** made over to him the ownership of the farm and seemed content to creep away to a corner and wait for death, he shrugged his shoulders and dismissed the old man from his mind.

   Sherwood Anderson, *Winesburg, Ohio*

a. The thunderstorm was the cause of something.
b. It had been sudden and fierce in downpour.
c. It brought to the fields the rain for the crops.
d. In addition, it was steady enough to remain in the parched land and penetrate to the roots.
e. The result was that the plants raised their branches.
f. Another result was that they arched their stems toward the sun.

4. *Model:* Warren McIntyre, **who casually attended Yale, being one of the unfortunate stags,** felt in his dinner-coat pocket for a cigarette and strolled out onto the wide, semi-dark veranda, where couples were scattered at tables, filling the lantern-hung night with vague words and hazy laughter.

F. Scott Fitzgerald, "Bernice Bobs Her Hair"

a. The sentence concerns Janice Larson.
b. She successfully finished auto-mechanics.
c. She had been one of few girls in the course.
d. She tried with great persistence for a related job.
e. In addition, she applied to several employment agencies.
f. At those agencies, counselors were surprised at her sex.
g. They described her prospects.
h. The description of her prospects was done with guarded optimism and sincere hope.

PRACTICING THE SKILL: SENTENCE COMBINING

PRACTICE 4

Following the structure of the model sentence, but using your own content, write a sentence imitation for each of the models below. Imitate the structure of the entire sentence, not just the S-V split.

1. The writer, **an old man with a white mustache,** had some difficulty in getting into bed.

Sherwood Anderson, *Winesburg, Ohio*

2. In the late afternoon Will Henderson, **owner and editor of the Eagle,** went over to Tom Willy's saloon.

Sherwood Anderson, *Winesburg, Ohio*

3. Yakov, **in loose clothes and peaked cap,** was an elongated nervous man with large ears, stained hard hands, a broad back and tormented face, lightened a bit by gray eyes and brownish hair.

Bernard Malamud, *The Fixer*

4. Over yonder, the Schenley, **in its vacant stretch,** loomed big and square through the fine rain, the windows of its twelve stories glowing like those of a lighted cardboard house under a Christmas tree.

Willa Cather, "Paul's Case"

5. The Russians, **coming from streets around the cemetery,** were hurrying, singly or in groups, in the spring snow in the direction of the caves in the ravine, some running in the middle of the slushy cobblestone streets.

Bernard Malamud, The Fixer

6. And so it was that Roberta, **after encountering Clyde and sensing the superior world in which she imagined he moved, and being so taken with the charm of his personality,** was seized with the very virus of ambition and unrest that afflicted him.

Theodore Dreiser, An American Tragedy

PRACTICE 5

In the first sentence in each pair, a slash mark (/) indicates that the writer's original sentence has an S-V split. Convert the other sentence into an S-V split that will fit smoothly into the place indicated by the slash mark. Compare your sentences with the originals in the References on page 155.

After you have combined the two sentences into one, write an imitation of the resulting sentence, using your own content but the structure of the model.

EXAMPLE

a. The Cavaliere, /, had lighted another cigarette.
b. The Cavaliere felt refreshed.

Combination with S-V Split

The Cavaliere, **refreshed,** had lighted another cigarette.

Thomas Mann, "Mario and the Magician"

Imitation

The jockey, **exhausted,** had won another race.

1a. The other sniper, /, thought that he had killed his man.

b. He thought so because he saw the cap and rifle fall.

Based on a sentence by Liam O'Flaherty, "The Sniper"

2a. Manuel, /, felt there was someone in the room.
b. Manuel was standing in the hallway.

Based on a sentence by Ernest Hemingway, "The Undefeated"

3a. The bull, /, pivoted and charged the cape, his head down, his tail rising.
b. The bull was in full gallop.

Based on a sentence by Ernest Hemingway, "The Undefeated"

4a. The members of the cuadrilla, /, came walking back and stood in a group talking, under the electric light in the patio.
b. The members had been watching the burlesque from the runway between the barrera and the seats.

Based on a sentence by Ernest Hemingway, "The Undefeated"

5a. He found that the older ones, /, were the easiest to handle.
b. Those who were easiest to handle were the ones who were running out of ideas and had taken to drink.

Based on a sentence by Roald Dahl, "The Great Automatic Grammatisator"

6a. A succession of loud and shrill screams, /, seemed to thrust me violently back.
b. These screams burst suddenly from the throat of the chained form.

Based on a sentence by Edgar Allan Poe, "The Cask of Amontillado"

PRACTICING THE SKILL: SENTENCE EXPANDING

PRACTICE 6

Add appropriate short S-V splits to each of the reduced sentences below. Each of the sentences in this group, in its original complete version, has short S-V splits—five words or fewer. When you finish, compare your sentences with the originals in the References on page 155. The place for your insert is indicated with a slash mark.

EXAMPLE

Reduced Sentence

A little house, /, appeared black in the distance.

Student-Expanded Sentence

A little house, **abandoned and overrun with weeds,** appeared black in the distance.

Original Sentence

A little house, **perched on high piles,** appeared black in the distance.

Joseph Conrad, "The Lagoon"

---

1. When the match went out, the old man, /, peeped into the little window.

Anton Chekhov, "The Bet"

2. The country house, /, was most enjoyable.

James Thurber, "Mr. Monroe Holds the Fort"

3. At once Buntaro slid an arrow from the quiver and, /, set up the bow, raised it, drew back the bowstring to eye level and released the shaft with savage, almost poetic liquidity.

James Clavell, Shogun

4. These three trains, /, confirmed my fears that traffic was not maintained by night on this part of the line.

Winston Churchill, "I Escape from the Boers"

5. The first opportune minute came that very afternoon, and Cress, /, went in tears to her room.

Jessamyn West, "Cress Delahanty"

6. And my departure, which, /, stank of betrayal, was my only means of proving, or redeeming, that love, my only hope.

James Baldwin, "Every Good-bye Ain't Gone"

7. Only a frying pan, /, remained.

Naomi Hintze, "The Lost Gold of Superstitions"

8. (Contains two.) His little dark eyes, /, and his mouth, /, made him look attentive and studious.

Albert Camus, Exile and the Kingdom

PRACTICE 7

Add appropriate longer S-V splits to each sentence below. Each of the sentences in this group, in its original complete version, has medium S-V splits—six to fifteen words. Compare your sentences with the originals in the References on page 156.

EXAMPLE

Reduced Sentence

There was also a rhino, who, /, came there each night.

Student-Expanded Sentence

There was also a rhino, who, **thirsty from having had no water since the rainy season a month ago,** came there each night.

Original Sentence

There was also a rhino, who, **from the tracks and the kicked-up mound of strawy dung,** came there each night.

Ernest Hemingway, *Green Hills of Africa*

---

1. During the first year of imprisonment, the lawyer, /, suffered terribly from loneliness and boredom.

Anton Chekhov, "The Bet"

2. While we were waiting for the coffee, the head waiter, /, came up to us bearing a large basket full of huge peaches.

W. Somerset Maugham, "The Luncheon"

3. Doubletree Mutt came sideways and embarrassed up through the vegetable patch, and Jody, /, put his arm about the dog's neck and kissed him on his wide black nose.

John Steinbeck, *The Red Pony*

4. Her gaze, /, changed the contour of her sallow-skinned face, skillfully re-fashioning her long-pointed nose on which a small chilly tear had gathered.

Brian Moore, *The Lonely Passion of Judith Hearne*

5. She, /, now gazed at him, fascinated by his enthusiasms.

Theodore Dreiser, *An American Tragedy*

6. The mouth-organist, /, got up and began dancing up and down the aisle, playing the instrument with one hand and flouncing up her skirts with the other as she jiggled in time to an old music-hall number....

Christy Brown, *Down All the Days*

7. Nick's heart, /, swelled with sweet thoughts of his wife and child, who lived in a foreign city across an ocean.

Edmund Ware, "An Underground Episode"

8. (Contains two.) And he, /, at once looked over his shoulder at her and, /, signaled that he would meet her.

Theodore Dreiser, *An American Tragedy*

PRACTICE 8

For each of the sentences below, provide three different expansions, as illustrated in the example. For each expansion, try to vary not only the

content but also the structure or combination of structures used in the
S-V split. Also, vary the length: some short, some medium, some long.
Punctuate correctly. Compare your sentences with the originals in the
References on page 157.

EXAMPLE

Reduced Sentence

That night after supper Mr. Delahanty, /, said to his wife, "I think
I'll just stay home and read tonight."

Sample Expansions

a. That night after supper Mr. Delahanty, **needing a night off
from party-going and social obligations to get ready for his
C.P.A. test,** said to his wife, "I think I'll just stay home
and read tonight."

b. That night after supper Mr. Delahanty, **who was nursing a
grudge against his wife caused by what he considered her
excessive gallivanting,** said, "I think I'll just stay home and
read tonight."

c. That night after supper Mr. Delahanty, **the classic example of
the home-body type husband who prefers to avoid the
discomforts of social occasions,** said to his wife, "I think
I'll just stay home and read tonight."

Original Sentence

That night after supper Mr. Delahanty, **who had been up at five,
irrigating, and who was put out with a climate so tardy with
its rains that irrigating this late in November was necessary,**
said to his wife, "I think I'll just stay home and read tonight."

Jessamyn West, "Cress Delahanty"

---

1. His face, /, felt more pleasure than pain in the wind and driving
snow.

Stephen Crane, "The Blue Hotel"

2. Once Enoch Bentley, /, struck his father, old Tom Bentley, with
the butt of a teamster's whip, and the old man seemed likely to
die.

Sherwood Anderson, *Winesburg, Ohio*

3. McCaslin, /, watched until the other's shadow sank down the wall

and vanished, becoming one with the mass of sleeping shadows.

William Faulkner, "Delta Autumn"

4. The big hands, /, hang loose off the wrist bone like clumsy, homemade tools hung on the wall of a shed after work.

Robert Penn Warren, "The Patented Gate and the Mean Hamburger"

5. (Contains two.) And Clyde, /, had not the courage or persistence or the background to go further with her now, went for his coat, and, /, departed.

Theodore Dreiser, An American Tragedy

PRACTICE 9

From a recent piece of writing of your own, select five sentences that don't have S-V splits. Add them.

11.

Sentence Closers

IDENTIFYING THE SKILL

Here's a list of sentences, all written by professional writers, but with some parts deleted.

1. It ran.
2. He strode forward.
3. He hung around L.A.
4. By and by, one group after another came straggling back to the mouth of the cave.
5. I would huddle.

Now compare the sentences above with the originals below. Notice that it's the **boldface** parts (sentence closers) that account for the professional sentence variety.

> **1a.** It ran, **its pelvic bones crushing aside trees and bushes, its taloned feet clawing damp earth, leaving prints six inches deep wherever it settled its weight.**
>
> Ray Bradbury, "A Sound of Thunder"

> **2a.** He strode forward, **crushing ants with each step, and brushing them off his clothes, till he stood above the skeleton, which lay sprawled under a small bush.**
>
> Doris Lessing, "A Sunrise on the Veld" from *African Stories*

> **3a.** He hung around L.A., **broke most of the time, working as an usher in movie theatres, getting an occasional part as an extra on the lots, or a bit on TV, dreaming and yearning and hungry, eating cold spaghetti out of the can.**
>
> John Dos Passos, "The Sinister Adolescents"

> **4a.** By and by, one group after another came straggling back to the mouth of the cave, **panting, hilarious, smeared from head to foot with tallow drippings, daubed with clay, and entirely delighted with the success of the day.**
>
> Mark Twain, *The Adventures of Tom Sawyer*

5a. I would huddle, **listening to their noise in the darkness, my eyebrows lifted, my lips pursed, the hair on the back of my neck standing up like pigs' bristle.**

John Gardner, *Grendel*

CHARACTERISTICS OF A SENTENCE CLOSER

Definition

A sentence closer is any structure or combination of structures that occupies the ending position of a sentence. Here are examples:

1. She often spoke of her life there, **living in luxury amidst plantations, servants, and saddle horses.**

Charles Spencer Chaplin (Charlie Chaplin), *My Autobiography*

2. The young white man who served us did it in leisurely fashion, **with long pauses for a smoke.**

Peter Abrahams, *Tell Freedom*

3. She returned to her bench, **her face showing all the unhappiness that had suddenly overtaken her.**

Theodore Dreiser, *An American Tragedy*

4. Bailey had graduated the year before, **although to do so he had had to forfeit all pleasures to make up for his time lost in Baton Rouge.**

Maya Angelou, *I Know Why the Caged Bird Sings*

5. He must conquer the snow, **this new, white brute force which had accumulated against him.**

D. H. Lawrence, "The Man Who Loved Islands"

Punctuation

In addition to any punctuation required within the sentence closer itself, a comma precedes it.

PRACTICING THE SKILL: SENTENCE SCRAMBLING

PRACTICE 1

Unscramble the sentence parts to produce a sentence with a sentence closer. Some sentences have more than one sentence closer; for those, decide the best order. Punctuate correctly. Compare your results with the originals in the References on page 157. Decide whether yours are as effectively organized as the professional writers'.

1a. limping
b. he went on.

William Faulkner, "Dry September"

2a. for what reason neither grand-parent would tell
b. from Grandpa
c. she was separated

Charles Spencer Chaplin (Charlie Chaplin), My Autobiography

3a. not rolling
b. it was a heavy sound
c. hard and sharp

Theodore Taylor, "The Cay"

4a. trying to be together as long as possible
b. and so we sent to the station, across the meadow
c. taking the longer way

Gerda Weissmann Klein, All But My Life

5a. and even changing the well-known scents
b. filling the whole room
c. sometimes a gaggle of them came to the store
d. chasing out the air

Maya Angelou, I Know Why the Caged Bird Sings

6a. a shadow
b. hour after hour
c. motionless
d. he stood there silent
e. carved in ebony and moonlight

James V. Marshall, Walkabout

7a. a gigantic race
b. before the creation
c. Prometheus was one of the Titans
d. who inhabited the earth
e. of man

Thomas Bulfinch, "Prometheus and Pandora"

8a. light flickered on bits of ruby glass
b. and on sensitive capillary hairs
c. in the nylon-brushed nostrils
d. on rubber-padded paws
e. its eight legs spidered under it
f. of the creature that quivered gently, gently

Ray Bradbury, Fahrenheit 451

PRACTICE 2

Each sentence below is a slightly scrambled version of a professional writer's sentence. In the original, there's a sentence closer. The scrambled version, however, has moved the sentence closer out of the ending position. Identify any structures that could become sentence closers and rearrange each sentence so that it has a sentence closer. Compare yours with the originals in the References on page 158. Which are better? Why?

Scrambled Sentences

1. Buck, the successful champion, the dominant primordial beast who had made his kill and found it good, stood and looked on.

   Jack London, *The Call of the Wild*

2. Hunched up under the blankets now, utterly relaxed, the Arab, his mouth open, was alseep.

   Albert Camus, "The Guest"

3. Buying furniture on the installment plan, being cheated and yet knowing no way to avoid it, that winter my mother and brother came, and we set up housekeeping.

   Richard Wright, *Black Boy*

4. Running hard, their heads down, their forearms working, their breath whistling, six boys, half an hour early that afternoon, came over the hill.

   John Steinbeck, *The Red Pony*

5. Somewhere, high above me, like some goddess whom I had discovered and regarded as my very own, she was always up there.

   Henry Miller, *Stand Still Like a Hummingbird*

6. On the stone floor of the pantry, face down, arms twisted at a curious angle, clad just in his vest and trousers, feet bare, Father lay crumped up.

   Christy Brown, *Down All the Days*

PRACTICING THE SKILL: SENTENCE IMITATING

PRACTICE 3

Underneath the model sentence are two imitations presented as a list of scrambled sentence parts for you to unscramble to duplicate the structure of the model. Unscramble each sentence to produce a sentence similar in structure to the model. Compare yours with the ones in the

References on page 158. The model sentence contains four sentence closers, three short, and one (the last) somewhat longer. The purpose of these sentence closers is to provide a specific description of the action stated in the main clause (*I would huddle*). The sentence closers are in **boldface**.

Model

> I would huddle, **listening to their noise in the darkness, my eyebrows lifted, my lips pursed, the hair on the back of my neck standing up like pigs' bristle.**
>
> <div align="right">John Gardner, <i>Grendel</i></div>

Scrambled Imitations

1a. deciding about their agenda for the sales meeting
  b. they would meet
  c. their opinions uncertain
  d. the leader of the group of section chiefs shouting out like a huckster
  e. their interest high

2a. their stems poised
  b. she smiled
  c. the arrangement of the bouquet of roses looking like a prize-winner
  d. their blossoms in full bloom
  e. glancing at the flowers in the vase

PRACTICE 4

First, read the model several times, paying special attention to the structure of the sentence. In each model the sentence closer is in **boldface**. Study it. Also, study the rest of the sentence carefully; you'll need to be familiar with not only the sentence closer but also the rest of the sentence structure.

Next, read the list of sentences underneath the model. Combine these into one sentence having the same (or similar) sentence structure as the model. Compare your sentences with the ones in the References on page 158.

Finally, write an imitation of the model, keeping the same structure as the model but providing your own content.

EXAMPLE

Model

Before she could put a stop to it, some of their classmates scoffed at the leaf-lard-and-black-bread sandwiches they ate for lunch, **huddled in one corner of the recreation room, dressed in their boiled-out ragpickers' clothes.**

Ambrose Flack, "The Strangers That Came to Town"

Sentences to Be Combined

a. Something happened when he selected a color for the sky.
b. One of his teachers commented on the bright hue.
c. The bright hue was the one he chose for backgrounds.
d. The bright hue was chosen with an aim.
e. The aim was toward a bold creativity.
f. The bright hue was applied.
g. The manner of application was with his most flamboyant brush strokes.

Combination

When he selected a color for the sky, one of his teachers commented on the bright hue he chose for backgrounds, **chosen with an aim toward a bold creativity, applied with his most flamboyant brush strokes.**

Imitation

If the needle damaged the surface of the record, several of the librarians complained about the scant concern borrowers gave to proper care, **governed only by their desire for enjoyment, unconcerned about their selfish carelessness.**

---

1. Model: Close to the village there lived a lady, **a small landowner who had an estate of about three hundred acres.**

Leo Tolstoy, "How Much Land Does a Man Need?"

a. This occurred high up the tree.
b. Some girls climbed there.
c. They were little adventurers.
d. They imagined a great escapade.
e. The escapade was of nearly Everest proportions.

2. *Model:* Touching the ropes and knots which joined the raft together, he stooped down, **his arms and shoulders buried under the cold water, and his chin kissing the rippling surface of the river.**

Shen T'Sung-Wen, "Under Cover of Darkness,"
translated by Y. Chia-Hua and Robert Payne

a. He was inspecting the plumbing and fixtures.
b. The plumbing and fixtures outfitted the new bathroom.
c. He walked around.
d. His tappings and probings were done.
e. They were done with his expert skill.
f. His experience was guiding his assessment.
g. The assessment was of the work.

3. *Model:* I could see the string of camels bearing the merchandise, and the company of turbaned merchants, **carrying some of their queer old firearms, and some of their spears, journeying downward toward the plains.**

Sir Rabindranath Tagore, "The Cabuliwallah"

a. They could foresee a time.
b. The time was of soldiers ending their battles.
c. They could foresee, in addition, a period of permanent truce.
d. They would be negotiating their disputes.
e. The disputes were about politics.
f. The disputes were about, in addition, many of the old arguments.
g. They would be living peacefully within dissent.

4. *Model:* Now it is night, and I am wrapped in a traveling rug on top of a four-in-hand coach, **driving with Mother and theatrical friends, cosseted in their gaiety and laughter as our trumpeter, with clarion braggadocio, heralds us along the Kennington Road to the rhythmic jingle of harness and the beat of horses' hoofs.**

Charles Spencer Chaplin (Charlie Chaplin), My *Autobiography*

a. Then it was graduation.
b. They were encouraged by a dream.
c. The dream was of new beginnings.
d. The new beginnings were for their lives.
e. They were marching among friends and proud parents.
f. They were dressed in their caps and gowns.
g. This all happened as the orchestra stirred them.
h. It stirred them with lusty fanfares.
i. It stirred them with its majesty of the pomp of trumpet blares.

j. It stirred them, in addition, with the circumstances of the formal right of passage.

PRACTICE 5

Following the structure of the model sentence, but using your own content, write a sentence imitation for each of the models below. Imitate the structure of the entire sentence, not just the sentence closer.

1. He has been lately confined to his bed, **because he was stricken by a severe case of dysentery.**

   Richard E. Kim, *Lost Names*

2. The children crawled over the shelves and into the potato and onion bins, **twanging all the time in their sharp voices like cigar-box guitars.**

   Maya Angelou, *I Know Why the Caged Bird Sings*

3. I enjoyed going to the shop, **even though we had to assemble and march out of the ghetto under guard, and be counted like cattle at departure and arrival.**

   Gerda Weissmann Klein, *All But My Life*

4. It had a black spot on it, **the black spot Mr. Summers had made the night before with heavy pencil in the coal-company office.**

   Shirley Jackson, "The Lottery"

5. As he ran away into the darkness, they repented of their weakness and ran after him, **swearing and throwing sticks and great balls of soft mud at the figure that screamed and ran faster and faster into the darkness.**

   Sherwood Anderson, *Winesburg, Ohio*

6. The strength that had been as a miracle in her body left, and she half reeled across the floor, **clutching at the back of the chair in which she had spent so many long days staring out over the tin roofs into the main street of Winesburg.**

   Sherwood Anderson, *Winesburg, Ohio*

PRACTICING THE SKILL: SENTENCE COMBINING

PRACTICE 6

In the first sentence in each group a slash mark indicates that the original sentence has a sentence closer. Convert the sentences underneath into a sentence closer that will fit smoothly into the place indicated by the slash mark. Compare your sentences with the originals in the References on page 159.

After you have combined the sentences into one, write an imitation of the resulting sentence, using your own content but the structure of the model.

EXAMPLE

a. It was falling on every part of the dark central plain, /, /, /, /.
b. It was falling on the treeless hills.
c. It was falling softly upon the Bog of Allen.
d. In addition, it was falling farther westward.
e. It was softly falling into the dark mutinous Shannon waves.

Combination with Sentence Closers

It was falling on every part of the dark central plain, **on the treeless hills, falling softly upon the Bog of Allen and, farther westward, softly falling into the dark mutinous Shannon waves.**

James Joyce, "The Dead"

Imitation

They were playing at various concerts of rock and roll, **at jammed theatres, entertaining powerfully in America and, even abroad, powerfully entertaining in sold-out European public halls.**

1a. I seemed forever condemned, /.
b. I was ringed by walls.

Based on a sentence by Richard Wright, Black Boy

2a. I waited for Andries at the back of the queue, /.
b. I was out of the reach of the white man's mocking eyes.

Based on a sentence by Peter Abrahams, Tell Freedom

3a. The Fog Horn was blowing steadily, /.
b. It was blowing once every fifteen seconds.

Based on a sentence by Ray Bradbury, "The Fog Horn"

4a. Gradually his head began to revolve, /, /.
b. It revolved slowly.
c. It revolved rhythmically.

Based on a sentence by D. H. Lawrence, "The Prussian Officer"

5a. Down on the little landing-bay were three cottages in a row, /, /.

b. The cottages were like coastguards' cottages.

c. The cottages were all neat and whitewashed.

Based on a sentence by D. H. Lawrence, "The Man Who Loved Islands"

6a. He spent long, silent hours in his study, /, /, /.

b. He was working not very fast.

c. Nor was he working very importantly.

d. He was letting the writing spin softly from him as if it were drowsy gossamer.

Based on a sentence by D. H. Lawrence, "The Man Who Loved Islands"

PRACTICE 7

Combine each list of sentences into one sentence containing a sentence closer(s). Underline the part of the resulting sentence that is the sentence closer(s). You may eliminate words, or change their form, so long as the intended meaning remains. Punctuate correctly. When you finish, compare your work with the original sentences in the References on page 159.

1a. The little boy stared at Ferris.

b. The little boy was amazed.

c. The little boy was, in addition, unbelieving.

Based on a sentence by Carson McCullers, "The Sojourner"

2a. I came out crawling.

b. I was clinging to the handle of the door.

c. I did all of this until I made sure of my bearings.

Based on a sentence by Richard E. Byrd, *Alone*

3a. Nick fought him.

b. The fighting was against the current.

c. Nick was letting him thump in the water.

d. The thumping in the water was against the spring.

e. The spring was of the rod.

Based on a sentence by Ernest Hemingway, "Big Two-Hearted River: Part II"

4a. Hattie sat down.

b. She sat at her old Spanish table.

c. She was watching them in the cloudy warmth of the day.

d. She was clasping her hands.

e. She was chuckling and sad.

Based on a sentence by Saul Bellow, "Leaving the Yellow House"

5a. Nick climbed out onto the meadow.

b. In addition, he stood.

c. Water was running down his trousers.

d. Water was running out of his shoes.

    e. His shoes were squlchy.

Based on a sentence by Ernest Hemingway, "Big Two-Hearted River: Part II"

6a. He walked with a prim strut.
  b. He was swinging out his legs.
  c. He swung them in a half-circle with each step.
  d. His heels were biting smartly.
  e. The biting was into the carpet.
  f. The carpet was red velvet.
  g. The carpet was on the floor.

Based on a entence by Carson McCullers, "The Jockey"

7a. The old woman slid to the edge.
  b. The edge was of her chair.
  c. She leaned.
  d. The leaning was forward.
  e. She was shading her eyes from the sunset.
  f. The sunset was piercing.
  g. She was shading her eyes with her hand.

Based on a sentence by Flannery O'Connor, "The Life You Save May Be Your Own"

Note: The sentence below contains sentence closers at the end of each of the two main clauses in the sentence.

8a. The horse galloped along wearily.
  b. The galloping was under the morning sky.
  c. The sky was murky.
  d. The horse was dragging his old rattling box after his heels.
  e. In addition, Gabriel was again in a cab.
  f. He was in there with her.
  g. They were galloping to catch the boat.
  h. They were galloping to their honeymoon.

Based on a sentence by James Joyce, "The Dead"

PRACTICING THE SKILL: SENTENCE EXPANDING

PRACTICE 8

Add appropriate sentence closers to each of the reduced sentences below. Each of the sentences, in their original complete versions, has sentence closers in the places indicated by slash marks. When you finish, compare your sentences with the originals in the References on page 159.

EXAMPLE

Reduced Sentence

We groped in the ruins and came upon this, and there he was, /, /, /.

Student-Expanded Sentence

We groped in the ruins and came upon this, and there he was, **a man about sixty, his clothes so neat that his attire contradicted his surroundings, a place for a gathering of derelicts.**

Original Sentence

We groped in the ruins and came upon this, and there he was, **sitting in his bunk, surrounded by foam and wreckage, jabbering cheerfully to himself.**

Joseph Conrad, "Youth"

---

1. She stood out from all the other girls in the school, /.

    Henry Miller, *Stand Still like a Hummingbird*

2. His face was fleshy and pallid, /.

    James Joyce, "The Dead"

3. The young white man who served us did it in leisurely fashion, /.

    Peter Abrahams, *Tell Freedom*

4. His earnestness affected the boy, /.

    Sherwood Anderson,*Winesburg, Ohio*

5. He was standing with her in the cold, /.

    James Joyce, "The Dead"

6. Mary Jane gazed after her, /, /.

    James Joyce, "The Dead"

7. As far down the long stretch as he could see, the trout were rising, /, /.

    Ernest Hemingway, "Big Two-Hearted River: Part I"

8. The girl at first did not return any of the kisses, but presently she began to, and after she had put several on his cheek, she reached his lips and remained there, /.

    Flannery O'Connor, "Good Country People"

REVIEW OF PROFESSIONAL SENTENCE VARIETY

PRACTICE 9

The professionally written sentences below illustrate the sentence positions in combination. Some contain sentence openers and S-V splits and sentence closers; others contain two of the three. Select any three model sentences. For each, construct a paragraph of from three to five sentences, one of which should be an imitation of one of the three model sentences you select from the list. The rest of the sentences in the paragraph should be written completely independent of model sentences. All of the sentences in each paragraph—not just the imitation of the model—should show mature sentence-composing style; otherwise, the imitation sentence will be grossly obvious. If you blend all the sentences, so that no one sentence stands out as superior in structure, you'll certainly have mastered the goal of this book: mature sentence structure.

EXAMPLE

Model

As we passed an open doorway, a huge dog came bounding out, **snarling and barking at us.**

Peter Abrahams, *Tell Freedom*

Limbering up on the floor of the practice room, they prepared for their next lesson on popular dances, tonight a variation on the three-step movement they had learned last week. **When the instructor entered from the faculty room, the students began livening up, bouncing and swaying to the stereo.** Without a word, he walked over to the corner of the mirrored room to the record player, switched it off, and then began dancing, with no music except the strong rhythm created by his moving body, his fluent choreography. The rest stood staring, entertained but a little envious, their feet tapping to his silent rhythm, fingers snapping to his body's pulse, waiting for him to give the signal to let them join in.

In this paragraph, all of the sentences, not just the imitation of the model, are competently written, with mature sentence structures that make it *impossible* to choose one sentence as the best.

The three paragraphs you write may be either consecutive—that is, all related in content—or separate, on three different topics. When you finish your paragraphs, exchange them with a classmate. If your classmate selects the sentence that was an imitation of a model, the rest of your sentences should be revised: they are inferior to the imitation. If the classmate is unable to choose one as the best, congratulations: all of your sentences resemble those of a professional writer.

Models

Choose one from each category: short, medium, long.

Short

1. He went on, **limping.**

   William Faulkner, "Dry September"

2. Yes, this man was fighting, **fighting with words.**

   Richard Wright, *Black Boy*

3. **At the gate,** I show the pass to a young Japanese private, **the sentry.**

   Richard E. Kim, *Lost Names*

4. **In an explosion of dirt and pebbles,** the pig burst from under the fence, **heaving Taran into the air.**

   Lloyd Alexander, *The Book of Three*

Medium

5. **Not knowing it,** we might kill an important animal, **a small bird, a roach, a flower even, thus destroying an important link in a growing species.**

   Ray Bradbury, "A Sound of Thunder"

6. **When she came into the wings,** she was very upset and argued with the stage manager who, **having seen me perform before Mother's friends,** said something about letting me go on in her place.

   Charles Spencer Chaplin (Charlie Chaplin), *My Autobiography*

7. His soul swooned slowly **as he heard the snow falling faintly through the universe and faintly falling, like the descent of their last end, upon all the living and the dead.**

   James Joyce, "The Dead"

8. **As he ran away into the darkness,** they repented of their weakness and ran after him, **swearing and throwing sticks and great balls of soft mud at the figure that screamed and ran faster and faster into the darkness.**

   Sherwood Anderson, *Winesburg, Ohio*

Long

9. Between each two rows of tubs in the center room were enormous whirling separators or dryers, **into which these webs of cloth, as they came from the tubs in which they had been shrinking for twenty-four hours, were piled and as much water as possible centrifugally extracted before they were spread out on the drying racks.**

Theodore Dreiser, An American Tragedy

10. **Standing in the truck bed, holding onto the bars of the sides,** rode the others, twelve-year-old Ruthie and ten-year-old Winfield, grime-faced and wild, their eyes tired but excited, their fingers and the edges of their mouths black and sticky from licorice whips, whined out of their father in town.

John Steinbeck, The Grapes of Wrath

11. The career of our play brought us through the dark muddy lanes behind the houses where we ran the gauntlet of the rough tribes from the cottages, **to the back doors of the dark dripping gardens where odours arose from the ashpits, to the dark odorous stables where a coachman smoothed and combed the horse or shook music from the buckled harness.**

James Joyce, "Araby"

12. Lil, **who would probably be just outside the gate with her boy,** would hear Father's voice and hurry in, **knowing he would vent his rage on Mother,** and almost as soon as she entered the kitchen she would be greeted with a fist or a lifted boot, and soon her rouge and mascara would be mingled with tears and blood as she wilted under a cascade of senseless violence, **not knowing why she was being beaten, knowing only the blows and curses and enraged bellowings raining down on her.**

Christy Brown, Down All the Days

The last sentence in this practice, which is also the last professionally written model sentence of SENTENCE COMPOSING was written by Christy Brown, a remarkable person who had to overcome incredible handicaps in order to begin the long process that eventually led to his becoming an outstanding writer. A victim of cerebral palsy, which prevented his using his hands and arms, he had to
learn to use his feet in order to write. Here's his account of his first attempt as a very young boy:

I tried again. I put out my foot and made a wild jerking stab with the chalk which produced a very crooked line and nothing more. Mother held the slate steady for me....

...I stiffened my body and put my left foot out again, for the third time. I drew one side of the letter. I drew half the other side. Then the stick of chalk broke, and I was left with a stump. I wanted to fling it away and give up. Then I felt my mother's hand on my shoulder. I tried once more. Out went my foot. I shook. I sweated and strained every muscle. My hands were so tightly clenched that my fingernails bit into the flesh. I set my teeth so hard that I nearly pierced my lower lip. Everything in the room swam till the faces around me were mere patches of white. But—I drew it—*the letter* "A." There it was on the floor before me. Shaky, with awkward, wobbly sides and a very uneven center line. But it *was* the letter "A." I looked up. I saw my mother's face for a moment, tears on her cheeks. Then my father stooped and hoisted me onto his shoulder.

Christy Brown, The Story of Christy Brown

The sentences Christy Brown went on to write, in such novels as *Down All the Days*, are literature at its finest. He learned how to write only through determination and practice, studying the writing of well-known authors.

Throughout this book, you've also practiced the skills professional writers use. If you keep consciously applying what you've learned to your own writing, you'll find yourself achieving a writing style that you can properly label "syntactically mature."

References

SENTENCE SCRAMBLING

PRACTICE 1 (pages 4-5)

1. When the ashtray, which was solid and feathered with grease, sang for him the dance of the petunia and became encouraged to jump up to an ocean and hope for mud, the crab blanked its pencil and covered the floor with its typewriters.
2. Although the hamburger, which was crystal and demented in town, ran down to him the story of the onion and seemed reluctant to fly away in a dictionary and study for words, the bun opened its halves and embraced the cheese in an instant.

PRACTICE 2 (pages 5-7)

Note: Nonsense versions may acceptably interchange some sentence parts.

1. Bob wrote his song, rehearsed it in the evenings, sang it beautifully in the play, but the small orchestra played with the beat ahead of the singer.
2. Snaze kurped its blander, broded it with the snart, crassed it frinkly from the marton, and the plimey peesto scrunted in the tunert of a bleepert.
3. To bring work from the office is to "relax" in a state of constant worry.
4. To jeld crams near town is to murd in a zipple from a zapple.
5. A sportscaster who communicates with fans and sports' top athletes is the choice announcer who communicates with great enthusiasm and with solid knowledge.
6. The blends which croak from selfhoose and their brained nabort are the best blends which croak near thirty bleeps and near forty bloops.

132

7. The wrinkled skin, very dry, yet with a softness about it as appealing as the sparkle in Grandma's eyes, shone in the candlelight.
8. An oversized saltert, quite pritert, and of a color on it as lumrious as a klanion in its woostem, plazoned from a yambrod.

PRACTICE 3 (pages 7-9)

1. He ran from the place, leaving his suitcase, leaving the quirt, leaving the oak box of money.
2. The father was respectable and tight, a mortgage financier and a stern, upright collection-plate passer and forecloser.
3. After Buck Fanshaw's inquest, a meeting of the short-haired brotherhood was held, for nothing can be done on the Pacific coast without a public meeting and an expression of sentiment.
4. With them, carrying a gnarled walking stick, was Elmo Goodhue Pipgrass, the littlest, oldest man I had ever seen.
5. He bounded out of bed wearing a long flannel nightgown over long woolen underwear, a nightcap, and a leather jacket around his chest.
6. Once upon a sunny morning a man who sat in a breakfast nook looked up from his scrambled eggs to see a white unicorn with a gold horn quietly cropping the roses in the garden.
7. Then, out of a box on the bed, she removed the gleaming pair of patent-leather dancing pumps, grabbed my right foot, and shoved it into one of them, using her finger as a shoehorn.

SENTENCE IMITATING

PRACTICE 1 (pages 10-11)

1. Different: b

Sources

a. Jack London, *All Gold Canõn*
b. Tate, "Ghost Men of Coronado"
c. Author

2. Different: b

Sources

a. Bernard Malamud, *The Assistant*
b. Ernest Hemingway, *Green Hills of Africa*
c. Author

3. Different: b

Sources

   a. Author
   b. Henry G. Felsen, "Horatio"
   c. John Steinbeck, "Flight"

4. Different: c

Sources

   a. Author
   b. Joseph Conrad, "The Idiots"
   c. William Faulkner, *Intruder in the Dust*

5. Different: b

Sources

   a. Author
   b. Ray Bradbury, *Fahrenheit 451*
   c. Aldous Huxley, *Antic Hay*

6. Different: a

Sources

   a. Ernest Hemingway, *For Whom the Bell Tolls*
   b. Author
   c. John Hersey, *Hiroshima*

SENTENCE COMBINING

PRACTICE 2 (pages 24-25)

1. The boy watched, his eyes bulging in the dark.
2. One of the dogs, the best one, had disappeared.
3. Jumping to his feet and breaking off the tale, Doctor Parcival began to walk up and down in the office of the *Winesburg Eagle* where George Willard sat listening.
4. This land was waterless, furred with the cacti which could store water and with the great-rooted brush which could reach deep into the earth for a little moisture and get along on very little.
5. It glided through, brushing the overhanging twigs, and disappeared from the river like some slim and amphibious creature leaving the water for its lair in the forests.

PRACTICE 3 (pages 25-26)

1. The country house, on this particular wintry afternoon, was most enjoyable.
2. The sun was setting when the truck came back, and the earth was bloody in its setting light.
3. He moves nervously and fast, but with a restraint that suggests that he is a cautious, thoughtful man.
4. The girls stood aside, talking among themselves, looking over their shoulders at the boys, and the very small children rolled in the dust or clung to the hands of their older brothers or sisters.
5. He took flour and oil, shaped a cake in a frying pan, and lighted the little stove that functioned on bottled gas.

PRACTICE 4 (pages 26-27)

1. From ten to fifteen he distributed handbills for merchants, held horses, and ran confidential errands.
2. Nick looked down into clear, brown water, colored from the pebbly bottom, and watched the trout keeping themselves steady in the current with wavering fins.
3. On one side, beginning at the very lip of the pool, was a tiny meadow, a cool, resilient surface of green that extended to the base of the frowning wall.
4. In the stillness of the air every tree, every leaf, every bough, every tendril of creeper and every petal of minute blossoms seemed to have been bewitched into an immobility perfect and final.

PRACTICE 5 (pages 27-29)

Paragraph One

(1) Manuel, leaning against the barrera, watching the bull, waved his hand, and the gypsy ran out, trailing his cape. (2) The bull, in full gallop, pivoted and charged the cape, his head down, his tail rising. (3) The gypsy moved in a zigzag, and as he passed, the bull caught sight of him and abandoned the cape to charge the man. (4) The gypsy sprinted and vaulted the red fence of the barrera as the bull struck it with his horns. (5) He tossed into it twice with his horns, banging into the wood blindly.

Paragraph Two

(1) To have a dance, the women sit in a circle with their babies asleep on their backs and sing medicine songs in several parts with falsetto voices, clapping their hands in a sharp, staccato rhythm at

counterpoint to the rhythm of their voices. (2) Behind their backs the men dance one behind the other, circling slowly around, taking very short, pounding steps which are again at counterpoint to both the rhythms of the singing and the clapping. (3) Now and then the men sing, too, in their deeper voices, and their dance rattles— rattles made from dry cocoons strung together with sinew cords and tied to their legs—add a sharp, high clatter like the sound of shaken gourds, very well timed because the men step accurately. (4) A Bushman dance is an infinitely complicated pattern of voices and rhythm, an orchestra of bodies, making music that is infinitely varied and always precise.

PRACTICE 6 (pages 30-31)

Paragraph One

(1) Outside, upon this lawn, stood an iron deer. (2) Further up on the green stood a tall brown Victorian house, quiet in the sunlight, all covered with scrolls and rococo, its windows made of blue and pink and yellow and green colored glass. (3) Upon the porch were hairy geraniums and an old swing which was hooked into the porch ceiling and which now swung back and forth, back and forth, in a little breeze. (4) At the summit of the house was a cupola with diamond leaded-glass windows and a dunce-cap roof!

Paragraph Two

(1) Upon the half decayed veranda of a small frame house that stood near the edge of a ravine near the town of Winesburg, Ohio, a fat little old man walked nervously up and down. (2) Across a long field that had been seeded for clover but that had produced only a dense crop of yellow mustard weeds, he could see the public highway long which went a wagon filled with berry pickers returning from the fields. (3) The berry pickers, youths and maidens, laughed and shouted boisterously. (4) A boy clad in a blue shirt leaped from the wagon and attempted to drag after him one of the maidens who screamed and protested shrilly. (5) The feet of the boy in the road kicked up a cloud of dust that floated across the face of the departing sun.

SENTENCE EXPANDING

PRACTICE 2 (pages 35-36)

1. She sprang dynamically to her feet, **clinching her hands,** then swiftly and noiselessly crossed over to her bed and, **from underneath it,** dragged out her suitcase.

2. He stood there, **rubbing his injured shoulder,** and Rainsford, **with fear again gripping his heart,** heard the general's mocking laugh ring through the jungle.

3. **Five, six, eight times,** he knocked the big man down, and the big man came again, **staggering, slavering, raving, vainly trying to rend and smash.**

4. We spent several evenings together, and the last one was the funniest, **because this time Joyce, who always had quite a lot to drink, got really potted.**

5. That night in the south upstairs chamber, **a hot little room where a full-leafed chinaberry tree shut all the air from the single window,** Emmett lay in a kind of trance.

6. **With something of the childish belief in miracles with which he had so often gone to class, all his lessons unlearned,** Paul dressed and dashed whistling down the corridor to the elevator.

PRACTICE 3 (pages 36-37)

1. On the outskirts of town, **she came upon her destination,** though at first she did not realize it.

2. **He stirred and drank it down,** sweet, hot, and warming in his empty stomach.

3. When the hostess saw that I was awake and that my safety belt was already fastened, **she smiled efficiently and moved on down the aisle,** waking the other passengers and asking them to fasten their safety belts.

4. Running up the street with all his might, **Marty could see that the game would start any minute now.**

5. Placing a cigarette between his lips, **he struck a match, inhaled the smoke hurriedly, and put out the light.**

6. At night, untired after the day's work, **he washed first in turpentine and then in water, and talked with the family.**

PRACTICE 4 (page 37)

1. In the hall stood an enormous truck, **behind the ladder that led to the roof, just opposite Hedger's door.**

2. All members of the staff, **from the ornithologists and researchers to the girls in the bookstore,** wore plastic tags bearing their names and color photographs.

3. Jerry stood on the landing, **smiling nervously.**

4. They lived in a square two-flat house tightly packed among identical houses on a fog-enveloped street in the Sunset district of San Francisco, **less than a mile from the ocean, more**

than three miles from Nob Hill, more than three thousand miles from Times Square.

5. His teeth, while strong and sharp, were, as weapons of offense, pitifully inadequate by comparison with the mighty fighting fangs of the anthropoids.

6. In the long, burning, murmurous Virginia summers, he used to ride, alone, back into the country towards the mountains, along the clay roads, dusty and red, and through the sweet-scented long grasses of the fields.

7. With an exclamation, she tossed her book to the deck, where it sprawled at a straddle, and hurried to the rail.

8. When one half of the world is angry at the other half, or one half of a nation is angry at the rest, or one side of town feuds with the other side, it is hardly surprising, when you stop to think about it, that so many people lose their tempers with so many other people.

PRACTICE 5 (page 38)

1. Standing in an aisle in a library, he can feel the eyes on him.

2. She made the best meatloaf in the world, and would give it to me raw, seasoned with onions and green peppers, from the bowl.

3. Now, lying in the ditch with Billy and the scouts after having been shot at, Weary made Billy take a very close look at his trench knife.

4. In the monastery where they stayed, Parador de San Francisco, the gardens were laid out so neatly, with fountains and stone benches, and stones inlaid on the walkways.

5. Above the open shirt, a pale silk scarf is tied around his neck, almost completely hiding from view the throat whose creases are the only sign of his age.

6. After this climax, the four animals continued to lead their lives, so rudely broken in upon by civil war, in great joy and contentment, undisturbed by further risings or invasions.

7. He went into the kitchen, where the moonlight called his attention to a half bottle of champagne on the kitchen table, all that was left from the reception in the tent.

SENTENCE COMPOSING WITH ABSOLUTE PHRASES

PRACTICE 1 (pages 42-43)

1. High in the air, a little figure, his hands thrust in his short

jacket pockets, stood staring out to sea. (S-V split)

2. He walked with a prim strut, swinging out his legs in a half-circle with each step, **his heels biting smartly into the red velvet carpet on the floor.** (sentence closer)
3. Outside, **his carpetbag in his hand,** he stood for a time in the barnyard. (sentence opener)
4. Father lay crumped up on the stone floor of the pantry, **[his] face down, [his] arms twisted at a curious angle....** **(sentence closers, with the possessive pronoun** *his* implied in each)

PRACTICE 2 (pages 43-44)

1. I was awake for quite a long time, thinking about things and watching Catherine sleeping, **the moonlight on her face.**
2. One of many small groups of children, **each child carrying his little bag of crackling,** we trod the long road home in the cold winter afternoon.
3. I looked across to a lighted case of Chinese design which held delicate-looking statues of horses and birds, small vases and bowls, **each set upon a carved wooden base.**

PRACTICE 3 (pages 44-45)

1. Then the rope tightened mercilessly while Buck struggled in fury, **his tongue lolling out of his mouth and his great chest panting.**
2. It ran, **its pelvic bones crushing aside trees and bushes, its taloned feet clawing damp earth,** leaving prints six inches deep wherever it settled its weight.
3. She was now standing arms akimbo, **her shoulders drooping a little, her head cocked to one side, her glasses winking in the sunlight.**
4. And then, **his feet sinking in the soft nap of the carpet, his hand in one pocket clutching the money,** he felt as if he could squeal or laugh out loud.
5. Within, you could hear the signs and murmurs as the furthest chambers of it died, **the organs malfunctioning, liquids running a final instant from pocket to sac to spleen, everything shutting off,** closing up forever.

PRACTICE 4 (page 45)

1. One customer in the line spoke out and ranted continuously about the unfair price, the other customers rallying and demanding the same reduction in the cost.

2. Several dancers near the band joined together and moved quick-ly into two lines, one couple heading and leading the rest through the complicated steps.

PRACTICE 5 (pages 45-47)

1. The youngest brother was nearby resting, **all his work over.**
2. As soon as it was over, they pranced around Gracie like courtiers, **Paul wooing her disgustingly with his stretched smiles.**
3. Later, somewhat sorry, he held the baby soothingly, and brought the music box to her and wound the toy up, **his voice singing with it.**
4. The student teacher erased everything quickly and, with a hurried cover-up, started to call out the spelling words for us, **her embarrassment definitely coming from her misspelling on the chalkboard.**

PRACTICE 7 (pages 48-49)

1. The town lay on a broad estuary, **its old yellow plastered buildings hugging the beach.**
2. Like giants they toiled, **days flashing on the heels of days like dreams as they heaped the treasure up.**
3. An Arab on a motorcycle, **his long robes flying in the wind of his speed,** passed John at such a clip that the spirals of dust from his turnings on the winding road looked like little tornadoes.
4. In solid phalanxes the leaders crowded about the three jaguars, **tusks thrust forward, their little eyes bloodshot with anger and with battle lust.**

PRACTICE 8 (page 50)

1. I could hear him crashing down the hill toward the sea, **the frightening laughter echoing back.**
2. Finny and I went along the Boardwalk in our sneakers and white slacks, **Finny in a light blue polo shirt and I in a T-shirt.**
3. All the time he was reading the newspaper, his wife, a fat woman with a white face, leaned out of the window, gazing into the street, **her thick white arms folded under her loose breast on the window sill.**
4. To the right of them the gym meditated behind its gray walls, **the high, wide, oval-topped windows shining back at the sun.**

PRACTICE 9 (pages 50-51)

1. Now, in the waning daylight, he turned into Glover Street toward his home, **his arms swinging as he moved onto the unpaved road.**

2. As they drove off Wilson saw her standing under the big tree, looking pretty rather than beautiful in her faintly rosy khaki, **her dark hair drawn back off her forehead and gathered in a knot low on her neck, her face as fresh, he thought, as though she were in England.**

3. His great chest was low to the ground, **his head forward and down, his feet flying like mad, the claws scarring the hard-packed snow in parallel grooves.**

4. In front of the house where we lived, the mountain went down steeply to the little plain along the lake, and we sat on the porch of the house in the sun and saw the winding of the road down the mountain-side and the terraced vineyards on the side of the lower mountain, **the vines all dead now for the winter** and **the fields divided by stone walls,** and below the vineyards, **the houses of the town on the narrow plain along the lake shore.**

PRACTICE 10 (page 51)

1. He began scrambling up the wooden pegs nailed to the side of the tree, **his back muscles working like a panther's.**

2. Touser roused himself under Fowler's desk and scratched another flea, **his leg thumping hard against the floor.**

3. They were smiling, **one woman talking, the others listening.**

4. Men, **their caps pulled down, their collars turned up,** swung by; a few women all muffled scurried along; and one tiny boy, **only his little black arms and legs showing out of a white wooly shawl,** was jerked along angrily between his father and mother; he looked like a baby fly that had fallen into the cream.

SENTENCE COMPOSING WITH APPOSITIVE PHRASES

PRACTICE 1 (page 55)

The appositive phrase is in **boldface.** Underlining indicates the word that the appositive phrase identifies.

1. The writer, **an old man with a white mustache,** had some difficulty in getting into bed. (S-V split)

2. Halfway there he heard the <u>sound</u> he dreaded, **the hollow, rasping cough of a horse.** (sentence closer)
3. <u>Mr. Mick Malloy,</u> **cashier at the Ulster and Connaught Bank,** draped his grey sports jacket neatly on a hanger and put on his black shantung work coat. (S-V split)
4. **A self-educated man,** <u>he</u> had accepted the necessary smattering facts of science with a serene indulgence, as simply so much further proof of what the Creator could do when He put His hand to it. (sentence opener)

PRACTICE 2 (page 56)

1. She struggled as usual to maintain her calm, composed, friendly bearing, **a sort of mask she wore all over her body.**
2. The judge, **an old, bowlegged fellow in a pale-blue sweater,** had stopped examining the animals and was reading over some notes he had taken on the back of a dirty envelope.
3. A man, **a weary old pensioner with a bald dirty head and a stained brown corduroy waistcoat,** appeared at the door of a small gate lodge.

PRACTICE 3 (pages 56-57)

1. One of them, **a slender young man with white hands, the son of a jeweler in Winesburg,** talked continually of virginity.
2. In the late afternoon Will Henderson, **owner and editor of the *Eagle*,** went over to Tom Willy's saloon.
3. The sound of the approaching grain teams was louder, **thud of big hooves on hard ground, drag of brakes,** and **the jingle of trace chains.**
4. Once Enoch Bentley, **the older one of the boys,** struck his father, **old Tom Bentley,** with the butt of a teamster's whip, and the old man seemed likely to die.
5. Mr. Mick Malloy, **tall, young secret gambler with devil-may-care eyes and a long humorous nose,** became Mr. Malloy, **tall cashier with a dignified face, a gentlemanly bank clerk, a nice sort of fellow.**

PRACTICE 4 (pages 57-58)

1. By the podium scholarly Henrietta stood, intelligent and composed and smiling, **president and valedictorian of the senior class.**
2. Under the canopy they danced, beaming and affectionate and happy, **bride and groom in their finery.**

PRACTICE 5 (pages 58-60)

1. Near the statue was an obvious tourist, **an oriental lady with a Kodak camera.**
2. *Gone with the Wind,* **the movie with the most re-issues,** originated as a novel of the old South by an unglamorous and unknown authoress.
3. "Missouri" is a special casserole, **a blend of potatoes and stewed tomatoes and hamburger.**
4. We were far from our destination and were making good time on the interstate, but no time to squander, and Dad wouldn't stop more than twice a day although we kids were itchy, and Mom, **a shrewd, gentle arbitrator with Solomon's mind,** circumvented some flare-ups, and those she couldn't she left to Heaven.

PRACTICE 7 (pages 61-62)

1. On this Sunday morning the postman and the policeman had gone fishing in the boat of Mr. Corell, **the popular storekeeper.**
2. The real estate agent, **an old man with a smiling, hypocritical face,** soon joined them.
3. They approached the domed synagogue with its iron weathercock, **a pock-marked yellow-walled building with an oak door,** for the time being resting in peace.
4. Lieutenant Tonder was a poet, **a bitter poet who dreamed of perfect, ideal love of elevated young men for poor girls.**

PRACTICE 8 (pages 62-63)

1. At the gate, I show the pass to a young Japanese private, **the sentry.**
2. When he was twelve, his mother married an executive of a machine tool company in Cleveland, **an engineer who had adult children of his own.**
3. **A modern intelligent woman,** my patient with her five children seemed in many ways as trapped as her forebears in Victorian times before the emancipation of women....
4. On the bark of the tree was scored the name of Deacon Peabody, **an eminent man,** who had waxed wealthy by driving shrewd bargains with the Indians.

PRACTICE 9 (pages 63-64)

1. Thus, one noontime, coming back from the office lunch down-

stairs a little earlier than usual, he found her and several of the foreign-family girls, as well as four of the American girls, surrounding Polish Mary, **one of the gayest and roughest of the foreign-family girls,** who was explaining in rather a high key how a certain "feller" whom she had met the night before had given her a beaded bag, and for what purpose.

2. The rest were standing around in hatless, smoky little groups of twos and threes and fours inside the heated waiting room, talking in voices that, almost without exception, sounded collegiately dogmatic, as though each young man, in his strident, conversational turn, was clearing up, once and for all, some highly controversial issue, **one that the outside, non-matriculating world had been bungling, provocatively or not, for centuries.**

3. Out in the distances the fans of windmills twinkled, turning, and about the base of each, about the drink tank, was a speckle of dark dots, **a gather of cattle grazing in moonlight and meditating upon good grass, block salt, impermanence, and love.**

4. Perhaps two or three times a year we would come together at a party, one of those teen-age affairs which last until dawn with singing and dancing and silly games such as "Kiss the Pillow," or "Post Office," **the game which permits one to call for the creature of one's choice and embrace her furtively in a dark room.**

PRACTICE 10 (page 64)

1. My bed was an army cot, **one of those affairs which are made wide enough to sleep on comfortably only by putting up, flat with the middle section, the two sides which ordinarily hang down like the sideboards of a drop-leaf table.**

2. He, **the enlightened man who looks afar in the dark,** had fled because of his superior perceptions and knowledge.

3. I had hardly any patience with the serious work of life which, not that it stood between me and desire, seemed to me child's play, **ugly monotonous child's play.**

4. There was Major Hunter, **a haunted little man of figures, a little man who, being a dependable unit, considered all other men either as dependable units or as unfit to live.**

SENTENCE COMPOSING WITH PARTICIPLE PHRASES

PRACTICE 1 (page 68)

The participle phrase is in **boldface**. <u>Underlining</u> indicates the word that the particple phrase modifies.

1. <u>Manuel,</u> **lying on the ground,** kicked at the bull's muzzle with his slippered feet. (S-V split)
2. **Clutching the clawing kitten to her collarbone,** her hair in her open mouth, <u>she</u> bawled encouragement to them. (sentence opener)
3. <u>They</u> were diggers in clay, **transformed by lantern light into a race of giants.** (sentence closer)
4. <u>Ruthie,</u> **dressed in a real dress of pink muslin that came below her knees,** was a little serious in her young-ladiness. (S-V split)

PRACTICE 2 (pages 69-70)

1. The author uses the S-V split position.

Sentence Opener Position (acceptable)

> **Wearing a black turtleneck sweater, dirty flannels, and slippers,** Bernard was waiting on the landing outside.

S-V Split Position (acceptable)

> Bernard, **wearing a black turtleneck sweater, dirty flannels, and slippers,** was waiting on the landing outside.

Sentence Closer Position (acceptable)

> Bernard was waiting on the landing outside, **wearing a black turtleneck sweater, dirty flannels, and slippers.**

2. The author uses the sentence opener position.

Sentence Opener Position (acceptable)

> **Sitting up in bed eating breakfast,** we could see the lake and the mountains across the lake on the French side.

S-V Split Position (acceptable)

> We, **sitting up in bed eating breakfast,** could see the lake and the mountains across the lake on the French side.

Sentence Closer Position (unacceptable)

> We could see the lake and the mountains across the lake on the French side, **sitting up in bed eating breakfast.**

3. The author uses the sentence opener position.

Sentence Opener Position (acceptable)

Coming down the pole, I had a sense of being whirled violently through the air, with no control over my movements.

S-V Split Position (acceptable)

I, **coming down the pole,** had a sense of being whirled violently through the air, with no control over my movements.

Sentence Closer Position (unacceptable)

I had a sense of being whirled violently through the air, with no control over my movements, **coming down the pole.**

4. The author uses the S-V split position.

Sentence Opener Position (acceptable)

Perched on high piles, a little house appeared black in the distance.

S-V Split Position (acceptable)

A little house, **perched on high piles,** appeared black in the distance.

Sentence Closer Position (unacceptable)

A little house appeared black in the distance, **perched on high piles.**

5. The author uses the sentence closer position.

Sentence Opener Position (unacceptable)

When we had made our way downstairs, **screaming and begging to be allowed to go with her mother,** we saw the woman with the lovely complexion, Miss Pilzer.

S-V Split Position (unacceptable)

When we had made our way downstairs, we, **screaming and begging to be allowed to go with her mother,** saw the woman with the lovely complexion, Miss Pilzer.

Sentence Closer Position (acceptable)

When we had made our way downstairs, we saw the woman with the lovely complexion, Miss Pilzer, **screaming and begging to be allowed to go with her mother.**

PRACTICE 3 (pages 70-71)

1. He was a blind beggar, **carrying the traditional battered cane and thumping his way before him with the cautious, half-furtive effort of the sightless.**
2. The passengers, **emerging from the mildewed dimness of the customs sheds, blinking their eyes against the blinding sunlight,** all had the look of invalids crawling into the hospital on their last legs.
3. That winter my mother and brother came, and we set up housekeeping, **buying furniture on the installment plan, being cheated, and yet knowing no way to avoid it.**
4. **Jumping to his feet and breaking off the tale,** Doctor Parcival began to walk up and down in the office of the *Winesburg Eagle,* where George Willard sat listening.
5. A young Mexican woman, **softened and dispirited by recent childbirth, dressed in the elegant, perpetual mourning of her caste,** came up slowly, **leaning on the arm of the Indian nurse who carried her baby,** his long embroidered robe streaming over her arm almost to the ground.

PRACTICE 4 (page 71)

1. As her arm whirled fast over the egg-whites, her face shifted toward the cookbook and stared at it, grimacing and expressing confusion and frustration over the third direction in the recipe that listed and explained more and ever more of the procedure.
2. After Jo-Jo climbed higher onto the counter, he pulled on the doors and looked for the candy, stretching but missing jars and boxes in the rear with bright colors that beckoned but hid farther and farther from his reach.

PRACTICL 5 (pages 71-73)

1. A pile of new debris cluttered up the driveway, and the tenants, **gazing at the disgrace,** watched with heavy hearts.
2. The dog sat up, his mouth clenching the rolled newspaper, **wagging his tail,** and begged a reward.
3. The upholstered pieces, the expensive, polished tables had been moved into the huge dining room, **covered with endless painter's cloths so that they would be protected from the splatterings of paint.**
4. The meeting that had been like a marathon among meetings continued, and the leader deliberated about his strategy, **stalling after the last remarks from the representative with whom**

he had planned so many emergency ploys focusing upon every conceivable tactic for the suppression of the opposition.

PRACTICE 7 (pages 75-77)

1. **Lying on the floor of the flat-car with the guns beside me under the canvas,** I was wet, cold, and very hungry.
2. There was a tattered man, **fouled with dust, blood, and powder stain from hair to shoes,** who trudged quietly at the youth's side.
3. I brought the boat up to the stone pier, and the barman pulled in the line, **coiling it on the bottom of the boat and hooking the spinner on the edge of the gunwale.**
4. The trail moved up the dry shale hillside, **avoiding rocks, dropping under clefts, climbing in and out of old water scars.**

PRACTICE 8 (page 77)

1. **Bleeding profusely and cut off from his supply of eagles' blood,** he had never been closer to death.
2. In an upstairs bedroom, shortly before dawn, a young American mother sat on the edge of a steel-framed bed, **rocking her nursing daughter.**
3. By and by, one group after another came straggling back to the mouth of the cave, **panting,** hilarious, **smeared from head to foot with tallow drippings, daubed with clay,** and **entirely delighted with the success of the day.**
4. Adolph Knipe took a sip of stout, **tasting the malty-bitter flavor, feeling the trickle of cold liquid as it traveled down his throat and settled in the top of his stomach,** cool at first, **then spreading and becoming warm, making a little area of warmness inside him.**

PRACTICE 9 (page 78)

1. With the core of the reel showing, his heart feeling stopped with excitement, **leaning back against the current that mounted icily up his thighs,** Nick thumbed the reel hard with his left hand.
2. Mrs. Carpenter was putting sun-tan oil on Sybil's shoulders, **spreading it down over the delicate, wing-like blades of her back.**
3. Soon the men began to gather, **surveying their own children, speaking of planting and rain, tractors and taxes.**

4. Lil, who would probably be just outside the gate with her boy, would hear Father's voice and hurry in, **knowing he would vent his rage on Mother,** and almost as soon as she entered the kitchen she would be greeted with a fist or a lifted boot, and soon her rouge and mascara would be mingled with tears and blood as she wilted under a cascade of senseless violence, **not knowing why she was being beaten, knowing only the blows and curses and enraged bellowings raining down on her.**

PRACTICE 10 (pages 78-79)

1. The children crawled over the shelves and into the potato and onion bins, **twanging all the time in their sharp voices like cigar-box guitars.**
2. And he, **sensing a new and strange and quite terrified note in all this the moment he read it,** at once looked over his shoulder at her and, **seeing her face so white and drawn,** signaled that he would meet her.
3. In the late afternoon, the truck came back, **bumping and rattling through the dust,** and there was a layer of dust in the bed, and the hood was covered with dust, and the headlights were obscured with a red flour.
4. He stood there, **balancing on one leg and holding tightly to the edges of the window sill with his hands,** staring at the sign and at the whitewashed lettering of the words.

REVIEWING AND APPLYING PROFESSIONAL SENTENCE STRUCTURES

PRACTICE 1 (pages 80-81)

1. Participle.
2. Appositive.
3. Participle (past).
4. Absolutes.
5. Absolutes.
6. Absolute.
7. Participle.
8. Participle (past).
9. Appositive.
10. Appositives.
11. Participles.
12. Appositives.

PRACTICE 4 (pages 84-86)

1. One participle, one absolute.
2. One absolute, one participle.
3. Two absolutes, one participle.
4. One appositive, one absolute.
5. One appositive, one absolute.
6. Two absolutes, one participle.
7. One absolute, one participle.
8. Two participles, one past and the other present.
9. One participle, two absolutes.
10. Three participles, one present and the others past.
11. One participle, one appositive.
12. One participle, one absolute.

PRACTICE 5 (pages 86-88)

1. The cat, **profiting by this unusual demonstration,** tried to effect an unnoticed retreat, and in doing so backed into the pickle-dish, which fell to the floor with a crash.
2. The eyes, **staring at the youth,** had changed to the dull hue to be seen on the side of a dead fish.
3. **Steeling himself against the first mouthful,** he dipped the spoon into the shimmering red liquid, lifted it to his lips.
   A red fountain splashed out in all directions, **staining the white table cloth.**
4. His body crumpled in like a leaf withered in sudden heat, and he came down, **his chest across his pan of gold, his face in the dirt and rock, his legs tangled and twisted because of the restricted space at the bottom of the hole.**
5. He knows that in spite of all the stout talk of his fellows he must live and die in uncertainty, **a thing blown by the winds, a thing destined like corn to wilt in the sun.**
   The eighteen years he has lived seem but a moment, **a breathing space in the long march of humanity.**

SENTENCE OPENERS

PRACTICE 1 (pages 91-92)

1. **Drifting into sleep,** he lost his balance, tipping backward again into memory.
2. **Without a word,** she takes a piece of paper out of her pants pocket.

3. **Even then, when we might have kissed and embraced unrestrainedly,** our shyness prevented us from sharing anything but the most innocent pleasure.

4. **Before the girls got to the porch,** I heard their laughter crackling and popping like pine logs in a cooking stove.

5. **When she came into the wings,** she was very upset and argued with the stage manager who, having seen me perform before Mother's friends, said something about letting me go on in her place.

6. **Being a star in her own right, earning twenty-five pounds a week,** she was well able to support herself and her children.

7. **Now, facing the bull,** he was conscious of many things at the same time.

8. **There, between two trees, against a background of gaunt black rocks,** was a figure from a dream, a strange beast that was horned and drunken-legged, but like something he had never even imagined.

PRACTICE 2 (page 93)

1. **At last, after what seemed hours,** my turn came.

2. **Behind and in front of us,** other children trotted in twos and threes.

3. **On the next try a few days later,** everything was perfect, even the punctuation.

4. **In the end, after several months of work,** he had persuaded something like seventy per cent of the writers on his list to sign the contract.

5. **Upon the half decayed veranda of a small frame house that stood near the edge of a ravine near the town of Winesburg, Ohio,** a fat little old man walked nervously up and down.

6. **Suffering, sick, and angry, but also grimly satisfied with his new stoicism,** he stood there leaning on his rifle, and watched the seething black mound grow smaller.

PRACTICE 3 (pages 93-94)

1. At the dumpster, when the truck arrived with junk, they emptied it out in minutes piling up the garbage, and as they pulled away and started the turn near Canal Street much too fast, the remaining debris began to clank in the back and near the cabin and to shift with thuds.

2. From the start, because the store had opened with haste, Jackson pondered constantly in dread during the day wondering about

his boss, and because he had been up late last night and had the alarm in the morning set too late, he dragged himself at eight o'clock to open up the store and the pre-payment office and to worry over his possible punishment.

PRACTICE 4 (pages 94-96)

1. **After meeting with the President,** he signed and delivered the letter to the secretary.
2. **After she tried the choreography,** she met the director, and they planned to confer with the producer.
3. **Through all the ups and downs of the trial,** the lawyers and the judge, the defendant and the jury, had been intense listeners to the expert testimony.
4. **Too pleasant to fight with the customer about the return, and too aggreeable to resist,** Miss Simpson agreed with a smile, refunded the money without protest, and remained remarkably calm.

PRACTICE 6 (pages 97-98)

1. **Within a week,** the manuscript had been read and accepted by an enthusiastic publisher.
2. **Like silent, hungry sharks that swim in the darkness of the sea,** the German submarines arrived in the middle of the night.
3. **Sitting beside his flowering window while the panes rattled and the wind blew in under the door,** Rosicky gave himself to reflection as he had not done since those Sundays in the loft of the furniture factory in New York, long ago.
4. **Crouched on the edge of the plateau,** the schoolmaster looked at the deserted expanse.
5. **And then, his feet sinking in the soft nap of the carpet, his hand in one pocket clutching the money,** he felt as if he could squeal or laugh out loud.
6. **Soiled by the filth of a strange city, spat upon by unknown mouths, driven from the streets into the roadway, carrying the heaviest loads upon his back, scurrying between carriages, carts, and horses, staring death in the eyes every moment,** he still kept silent.

PRACTICE 7 (pages 98-100)

1. **Remaining single,** a man converts himself into a permanent public temptation.

2. **Pain shooting up my entire arm,** I lay panting on the edge of the pool and gingerly began to feel my wrist.
3. **Pretending to take an interest in the New Season's Models,** Gumbril made, squinting sideways over the burning tip of his cigar, an inventory of her features.
4. **In the frosty December dusk,** their cabins looked neat and snug with pale blue smoke rising from the chimneys and doorways glowing amber from the fires inside.
5. **In the darkness in the hallway by the door,** the sick woman arose and started again toward her own room.
6. **In her girlhood and before her marriage with Tom Willard,** Elizabeth had borne a somewhat shaky reputation in Winesburg.
7. **Near the edge of town,** the group had to walk around an automobile burned and squatting on the narrow road, and the bearers on one side, unable to see their way in the darkness, fell into a deep ditch.
8. **By nightfall of an average courting day,** a fiddler crab who has been standing on tiptoe for eight or ten hours waving a heavy claw in the air is in pretty sad shape.

PRACTICE 8 (pages 100-101)

1. **When Hedger came slinking out of his closet,** he sat down on the edge of the couch, sat for hours without moving.
2. **As she grew older and handsomer,** she had many beaux, but these small-town boys didn't interest her.
3. **In her own mind,** the tall dark girl had been in those days much confused.
4. **To a man so newly lonely, so newly alone,** an invitation out meant an evening in other people's lives, and therefore freedom from his own, and it meant the possibility of laughter that would surprise him—how good it was to be alive and healthy, to have a body that had not given up in spite of everything.
5. **In the late afternoon,** the truck came back, bumping and rattling through the dust, and there was a layer of dust in the bed, and the hood was covered with dust, and the headlights were obscured with a red flour.
6. **When the night crept down in shadowy blue and silver,** they threaded the shimmering channel in the rowboat and, tying it to a jutting rock, began climbing the cliff together.
7. **Whenever she lay awake beside her husband, like tonight,** she would still keep her eyes closed for a long time, then open them and relish with astonishment the blue of the brand-

SENTENCE COMPOSING

new curtains, replacing the apricot-pink which had filtered with the morning light into the room where she had slept as a girl.

8. **Tugged here and there in his stockinged feet, bewildered by the numbers, staggered by so much raw flesh,** Dr. Sasaki lost all sense of profession and stopped working as a skillful surgeon and a sympathetic man; he became an automaton, mechanically wiping, daubing, winding, wiping, daubing, winding.

S-V SPLITS

PRACTICE 1 (pages 105-106)

1. The writer, **an old man with a white mustache,** had some difficulty in getting into bed.
2. When Jesse Bentley, **absorbed in his own idea,** suddenly arose and advanced toward him, his terror grew until his whole body shook.
3. The twins, **smeary in the face, eating steadily from untidy paper sacks of sweets,** followed them in a detached way.
4. His hands, **beyond control,** ran up and down the soft-skinned baby body, the sinuous, limbless body.
5. One of them, **a slender young man with white hands, the son of a jeweler in Winesburg,** talked continually of virginity.
6. His face, **fresh from the pounding of Johnnie's fists,** felt more pleasure than pain in the wind and the driving snow.
7. The big hands, **with the knotted, cracked joints and the square, horn-thick nails,** hang loose off the wrist bone like clumsy, homemade tools hung on the wall of a shed after work.
8. The four pretty, slatternly Spanish girls, **their dark hair sleeked down over their ears, their thin-soled black slippers too short in the toes and badly run over at high heels,** took leisurely leave, with kisses all around, of a half dozen local young men, who had brought flowers and baskets of fruit.

PRACTICE 2 (pages 106-107)

1. In the flurry of traffic, the ambulance driver, **who only an hour ago had been asleep,** gripped the steering wheel, and his siren, **wailing like a giant in agony,** warned the traffic to make way.
2. Near the field of wheat, tough-skinned Jasper, **who a year ago had been an irresponsible drunk,** walked peacefully among

his crops, and his serenity, **derived from his year's self-control with alcohol,** allowed him to concentrate on farming.

PRACTICE 3 (pages 107-109)

1. Nielsen Rating Service, **a determiner of TV ratings which had been accepted by the TV networks that season,** was surveying this morning.
2. The cook, **a fine-bellied gourmet,** was back in the kitchen at the closet freezer, ruminating about the latest beef selections, but the butcher reassured him.
3. Because the thunderstorm, **which was sudden and fierce in downpour,** brought to fields the rain for the crops and was steady enough to remain in the parched land and penetrate to the roots, the plants raised their branches and arched their stems toward the sun.
4. Janice Larson, **who successfully finished auto-mechanics, having been one of few girls in the course,** tried with great persistence for a related job and applied to several employment agencies, where counselors were surprised at her sex, describing her prospects with guarded optimism and sincere hope.

PRACTICE 5 (pages 110-111)

1. The other sniper, **seeing the cap and rifle fall,** thought that he had killed his man.
2. Manuel, **standing in the hallway,** felt there was someone in the room.
3. The bull, **in full gallop,** pivoted and charged the cape, his head down, his tail rising.
4. The members of the cuadrilla, **who had been watching the burlesque from the runway between the barrera and the seats,** came walking back and stood in a group talking, under the electric light in the patio.
5. He found that the older ones, **those who were running out of ideas and had taken to drink,** were the easiest to handle.
6. A succession of loud and shrill screams, **bursting suddenly from the throat of the chained form,** seemed to thrust me violently back.

PRACTICE 6 (pages 111-112)

1. When the match went out, the old man, **trembling from agitation,** peeped into the little window.
2. The country house, **on this particular wintry afternoon,** was most enjoyable.

3. At once Buntaro slid an arrow from the quiver and, **still sitting,** set up the bow, raised it, drew back the bowstring to eye level and released the shaft with savage, almost poetic liquidity.
4. These three trains, **motionless in the moonlight,** confirmed my fears that traffic was not maintained by night on this part of the line.
5. The first opportune minute came that very afternoon, and Cress, **after being warned,** went in tears to her room.
6. And my departure, which, **especially in my own eyes,** stank of betrayal, was my only means of proving, or redeeming, that love, my only hope.
7. Only a frying pan, **with an arrow through it,** remained.
8. His little dark eyes, **deepset under a tanned forehead,** and his mouth, **surrounded with wrinkles,** made him look attentive and studious.

PRACTICE 7 (pages 112-113)

1. During the first year of imprisonment, the lawyer, **as far as it was possible to judge from his short notes,** suffered terribly from loneliness and boredom.
2. While we were waiting for the coffee, the headwaiter, **with an ingratiating smile on his false face,** came up to us bearing a large basket full of huge peaches.
3. Doubletree Mutt came sideways and embarrassed up through the vegetable patch, and Jody, **remembering how he had thrown the clod,** put his arm about the dog's neck and kissed him on his wide black nose.
4. Her gaze, **deceiving, transforming her to her imaginings,** changed the contour of her sallow-skinned face, skillfully re-fashioning her long-pointed nose on which a small chilly tear had gathered.
5. She, **thrilled and in part seduced by his words, instead of resisting as definitely as she would have in any other case,** now gazed at him, fascinated by his enthusiasms.
6. The mouth-organist, **now revealed as a motherly middle-aged woman with a large and rather dignified wart on her nose,** got up and began dancing up and down the aisle, playing the instrument with one hand and flouncing up her skirts with the other as she jiggled in time to an old music-hall number....
7. Nick's heart, **under the bone and muscle of his great chest,** swelled with sweet thoughts of his wife and child, who lived in a foreign city across an ocean.
8. And he, **sensing a new and strange and quite terrified note**

in all this the moment he read it, at once looked over his shoulder at her and, **seeing her face so white and drawn,** signaled that he would meet her.

PRACTICE 8 (pages 113-115)

1. His face, **fresh from the pounding of Johnnie's fists,** felt more pleasure than pain in the wind and the driving snow.
2. Once Enoch Bentley, **the older one of the boys,** struck his father, old Tom Bentley, with the butt of a teamster's whip, and the old man seemed likely to die.
3. McCaslin, **still propped on his elbow,** watched until the other's shadow sank down the wall and vanished, becoming one with the mass of sleeping shadows.
4. The big hands, **with the knotted, cracked joints and the square, horn-thick nails,** hang loose off the wrist bone like clumsy, homemade tools hung on the wall of a shed after work.
5. And Clyde, **realizing that for some reason he must not say more,** had not the courage or persistence or the background to go further with her now, went for his coat, and, **looking sadly but obediently back at her,** departed.

SENTENCE CLOSERS

PRACTICE 1 (pages 117-118)

1. He went on, **limping.**
2. She was separated from Grandpa, **for what reason neither grand-parent would tell.**
3. It was a heavy sound, **hard and sharp, not rolling.**
4. And so we went to the station, across the meadow, **taking the longer way, trying to be together as long as possible.**
4. Sometimes a gaggle of them came to the Store, **filling the whole room, chasing out the air and even changing the well-known scents.**
6. Hour after hour he stood there silent, **motionless, a shadow carved in ebony and moonlight.**
7. Prometheus was one of the Titans, **a gigantic race who inhabited the earth before the creation of man.**
8. Light flickered on bits of ruby glass and on sensitive capillary hairs in the nylon-brushed nostrils of the creature that quivered gently, gently, **its eight legs spidered under it on rubber-padded paws.**

PRACTICE 2 (page 119)

1. Buck stood and looked on, **the successful champion, the dominant primordial beast who had made his kill and found it good.**

2. The Arab was asleep, **hunched up near the blankets now, his mouth open, utterly relaxed.**

3. That winter my mother and brother came, and we set up housekeeping, **buying furniture on the installment plan, being cheated and yet knowing no way to avoid it.**

4. Six boys came over the hill, **half an hour early that afternoon, running hard, their heads down, their forearms working, their breath whistling.**

5. She was always up there somewhere, **high above me, like some goddess whom I had discovered and regarded as my very own.**

6. Father lay crumped up on the stone floor of the pantry, **face down, arms twisted at a curious angle, clad just in his vest and trousers, feet bare.**

PRACTICE 3 (pages 119-120)

1. They would meet, **deciding about their agenda for the sales meeting, their opinions uncertain, their interest high, the leader of the group of section chiefs shouting out like a huckster.**

2. She smiled, **glancing at the flowers in the vase, their stems poised, their blossoms in full bloom, the arrangement of the bouquet of roses looking like a prize-winner.**

PRACTICE 4 (pages 120-123)

1. High up the tree there climbed some girls, **little adventurers who imagined a great escapade of nearly Everest proportions.**

2. Inspecting the plumbing and fixtures that outfitted the new bathroom, he walked around, **his tappings and probings done with his expert skill, and his experience guiding his assessment of the work.**

3. They could foresee a time of soldiers ending their battles, and a period of permanent truce, **negotiating their disputes about politics, and many of the old arguments, living peacefully within dissent.**

4. Then it was graduation, and they were encouraged by a dream of new beginnings for their lives, **marching among friends and**

proud parents, dressed in their caps and gowns as the orchestra, with lusty fanfares, stirred them with its majesty of the pomp of trumpet blares and the circumstances of the formal rite of passage.

PRACTICE 6 (pages 123-125)

1. I seemed forever condemned, **ringed by walls.**
2. I waited for Andries at the back of the queue, **out of the reach of the white man's mocking eyes.**
3. The Fog Horn was blowing steadily, **once every fifteen seconds.**
4. Gradually his head began to revolve, **slowly, rhythmically.**
5. Down on the little landing-bay were three cottages in a row, **like coast-guards' cottages, all neat and whitewashed.**
6. He spent long, silent hours in his study, **working not very fast, nor very importantly, letting the writing spin softly from him as if it were drowsy gossamer.**

PRACTICE 7 (pages 125-126)

1. The little boy stared at Ferris, **amazed and unbelieving.**
2. I came out crawling, **clinging to the handle of the door until I made sure of my bearings.**
3. Nick fought him against the current, **letting him thump in the water against the spring of the rod.**
4. Hattie sat down at her old Spanish table, **watching them in the cloudly warmth of the day, clasping her hands, chuckling and sad.**
5. Nick climbed out onto the meadow and stood, **water running down his trousers and out of his shoes, his shoes squlchy.**
6. He walked with a prim strut, **swinging out his legs in a half-circle with each step, his heels biting smartly into the red velvet carpet on the floor.**
7. The old woman slid to the edge of her chair and leaned forward, **shading her eyes from the piercing sunset with her hand.**
8. The horse galloped along wearily under the murky morning sky, **dragging his old rattling box after his heels,** and Gabriel was again in a cab with her, **galloping to catch the boat, galloping to their honeymoon.**

PRACTICE 8 (pages 126-127)

1. She stood out from all the other girls in the school, **like someone with blue blood in her veins.**

2. His face was fleshy and pallid, **touched with colour only at the thick hanging lobes of his ears and at the wide wings of his nose.**

3. The young white man who served us did it in leisurely fashion, **with long pauses for a smoke.**

4. His earnestness affected the boy, **who presently became silent and a little alarmed.**

5. He was standing with her in the cold, **looking in through a grated window at a man making bottles in a roaring furnace.**

6. Mary Jane gazed after her, **a moody puzzled expression on her face, while Mrs. Conroy leaned over the banisters to listen for the hall-door.**

7. As far down the long stretch as he could see, the trout were rising, **making circles all down the surface of the water, as though it were starting to rain.**

8. The girl at first did not return any of the kisses, but presently she began to, and after she had put several on his cheek, she reached his lips and remained there, **kissing him again and again as if she were trying to draw all the breath out of him.**